KiddiWalks
IN BERKSHIRE

Ruth Paley

COUNTRYSIDE BOOKS
NEWBURY BERKSHIRE

COUNTRYSIDE BOOKS
3 Catherine Road
Newbury, Berkshire

To view our complete range of books,
please visit us at
www.countrysidebooks.co.uk

ISBN 978 1 84674 239 2

For RACHAEL, JACOB AND JESSICA

Cover design by Jan Marshall
Cover picture © Christophe.rolland1/Dreamstime.com

Designed by Peter Davies, Nautilus Design
Produced through MRM Associates Ltd., Reading
Printed by Information Press, Oxford

Contents

Contents

PUBLISHER'S NOTE

We hope that you obtain considerable enjoyment from this book; great care has been taken in its preparation. Although at the time of publication all routes followed public rights of way or permitted paths, diversion orders can be made and permissions withdrawn.

We cannot, of course, be held responsible for such diversion orders and any inaccuracies in the text which result from these or any other changes to the routes nor any damage which might result from walkers trespassing on private property. We are anxious though that all details covering the walks are kept up to date and would therefore welcome information from readers which would be relevant to future editions.

The simple sketch maps that accompany the walks in this book are based on notes made by the author whilst checking out the routes on the ground. They are designed to show you how to reach the start, to point out the main features of the overall circuit and they contain a progression of numbers that relate to the paragraphs of the text.

Introduction

Berkshire is a beautiful county to explore with your children, with the North Wessex Downs a designated Area of Outstanding Natural Beauty. It is also one of the smallest counties in England and has the M4 and A4 running straight across it, which makes it quick and easy to get from one place to another and explore somewhere different. This book has 20 suggestions for family days out across the county. On a family walk, children can learn to appreciate the countryside and wildlife, as well as learning about the history of the area they live in.

These walks have been designed specifically for children and each route includes *Background Notes* that tell you something about the history, geology or wildlife of the area you are walking through while *Fun Things to See and Do* adds to the adventure by suggesting things for the children to spot, play areas or something to discover along the way. My children are always much more enthusiastic walkers if we meet up with friends. A group of children will charge down a towpath or across fields for miles without any signs of tiring out. So pack a picnic and an OS map and meet some friends for a free adventure exploring the beautiful countryside on your doorstep.

These walks lead you up to the rolling downland by West Ilsley, through pretty villages, copses and fields by Yattendon and Hampstead Norreys, to native woodland filled with songbirds and wildflowers at Bowdown and Moor Copse. Walks along the towpath by the Kennet and Avon Canal in Hungerford and Kintbury are always popular with children as you can feed the ducks and watch the colourful narrowboats. Around Theale, former gravel pits have filled with water to become tranquil nature reserves for water birds. Hosehill Lake and Loddon are two lakeside walks where children can see lots of different types of birds, as well as dragonflies and butterflies in summer. Walking in a nature reserve is always a good option for children, which is why I have included four walks on land owned by the Berkshire, Buckinghamshire and Oxfordshire Wildlife Trust. The Wildlife Trust provides excellent information boards and clear paths so children can run around and explore without worrying about traffic or getting lost. The River Thames is at its most beautiful as it snakes through ancient water meadows by Cookham. This scenery was

Kiddiwalks in Berkshire

the inspiration for Kenneth Grahame when he wrote *The Wind in the Willows*, while the Thames at Pangbourne provided the backdrop for Ernest H. Shepard's beautiful illustrations, which helped to turn the book into an enduring children's classic. Following the Thames east takes you through Royal Windsor and Eton, steeped in history with a fairytale castle and changing of the guard for children to wonder at.

I have loved discovering Berkshire with my three children aged 5, 7 and 9, who have enthusiastically tested out each walk. They have charged up and down a Norman motte, played gladiators in a Roman amphitheatre, watched the swans by the River Thames and spotted skylarks singing above them. So I would like to say the biggest thank you to Rachael, Jacob and Jessica for walking across Berkshire in sunshine and rain, and to my husband Matt for always carrying the rucksack.

Ruth Paley

AREA MAP SHOWING THE LOCATIONS OF THE WALKS

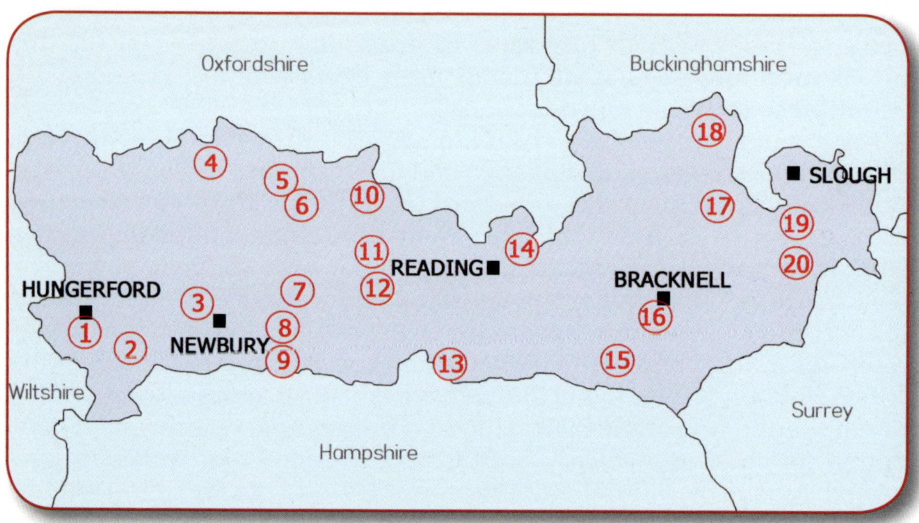

Hungerford Marsh

Who's for a Game of Pooh Sticks?

A frosty morning at Hungerford Marsh

This peaceful ramble takes you through two beautiful nature reserves. As you are always by water, it is an ideal walk for a hot summer's day, although the wonderful variety of birds that live here gives this pretty circuit year-round interest. Children will love following the shallow river round the nature reserve, with little bridges along the way that are perfect for Pooh sticks. St Lawrence's church tower is always visible on the horizon and the marsh is a picturesque mix of water meadows and reedbeds, with yellow iris and southern marsh-orchids in the summer, marsh-marigold and ragged-robin in the spring.

Getting there Follow the A4 into Hungerford and at the roundabout by the Bear Hotel turn into Bridge Street. Turn right at the next roundabout into Church Street then right onto Parsonage Lane. This narrow lane leads you under a railway bridge to St Lawrence's church. From Hungerford train station, walk to the bridge, turn left and follow the towpath until you reach the church and the start of the walk.

Length of walk 1½ miles.
Time 1 hour.
Terrain Easy walking on flat, grassy paths and towpath.

Start/Parking On the roadside in front of St Lawrence's church (GR: SU 334687).
Map OS Explorer 158 Newbury & Hungerford.
Refreshments Hungerford has plenty of tearooms and pubs. The Tutti Pole by the bridge sells delicious ice creams and there are benches by the canal where you can sit and watch the ducks. Alternatively, bring a picnic and eat it by Ash Pool.

The Walk

1 Follow the public footpath by the left side of the churchyard, which is filled with snowdrops in early spring. The path leads to the towpath by the Kennet and Avon Canal. Cross the wooden

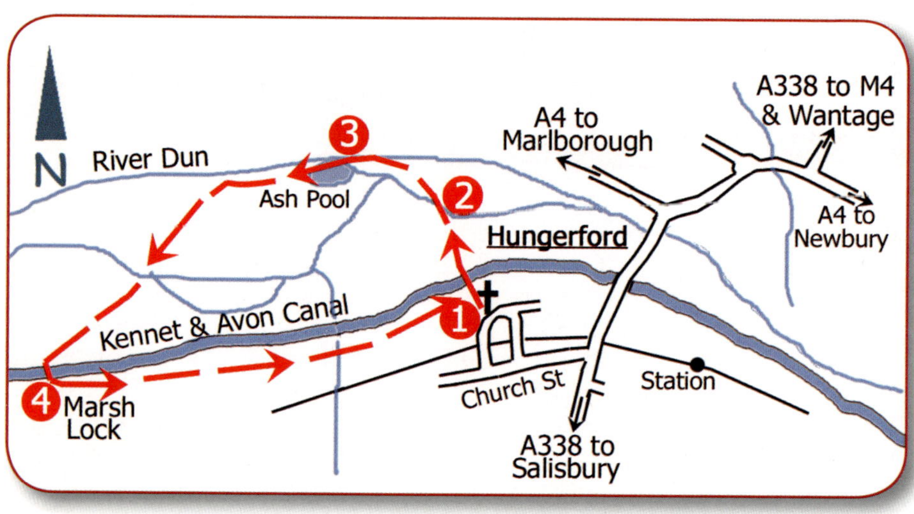

bridge directly in front of you and go through a kissing gate into Hungerford Marsh Nature Reserve. There is a short path to another swing gate and a narrow footbridge over the fast-flowing River Shalbourne, a perfect spot for Pooh sticks.

2 Cross the bridge and go through another gate to follow the path left, with the clear waters of the River Dun on your right. In summer there are reeds either side of the path. Continue straight on and through a kissing gate into Freeman's Marsh. There is an information board here with a map and notes on the wildlife and history of the area.

3 Follow the path, with Ash Pool on your left, to another narrow footbridge. Cross and go through the swing gate. The River Dun becomes wider along this stretch and is fenced off from the path to protect the banks from the cattle; look out for wild brown trout in the water. You can see a public footpath sign ahead of you. At this point turn left, leaving the river behind you and follow the grassy path half left across the marsh to a narrow iron footbridge. Cross the bridge, then follow the path right to cross the bridge at Marsh Lock. Be careful here as there is deep water in the lock.

4 Turn left and go down the grassy slope to follow the Kennet and Avon Canal towpath back towards the church. There is a railway track on your right, and although you can't see the track, children will enjoy spotting the occasional train hurtling past on the London to Bristol line. Pass another information sign about Freeman's Marsh and go

◆ Fun Things to See and Do ◆

The narrow footbridges in the nature reserve are perfect for **Pooh sticks**. Get a twig and line up on the bridge, then all at the same time drop your twigs into the river. Whip round and see whose twig races under the bridge first. The shallow waters of Ash Pool are perfect for **paddling and pond dipping**. Bring a net and bucket and see what you can find. Make sure you empty the bucket back into the pool when you've finished.

through the gate, leaving the nature reserve behind you. There are often fishermen sitting along this stretch of the canal, with tubs filled with wriggling bait, as well as colourful narrowboats to spot. Soon you will recognise the bridge you crossed at the start of the walk and turn right, back through the churchyard.

Paddling in the shallow waters of Ash Pool

◆ Background Notes ◆

Hungerford dates back to Saxon times and is well worth a visit. There are small independent shops to explore, including an old-fashioned sweet shop and toy shop, as well as many antique shops. Hungerford Arcade is filled with curios that children will find fascinating, ranging from old telephones and coins to medals and Corgi cars.

In 1688, during the 'Glorious Revolution', William of Orange stayed at the 13th-century **Bear Inn** in Hungerford as he travelled from Devon to London. William was the Protestant husband of Mary, King James II's eldest daughter. Upon the birth of a Catholic son and heir to the unpopular James II, William was invited by disgruntled Protestant nobles to invade England. William met with James II's commissioners at the Bear Inn and, days later, James fled to France, throwing the Great Seal of England into the River Thames on the way.

Kintbury

Ducks and Narrowboats

Feeding the swans on the Kennet and Avon Canal

This is a picturesque route along the towpath of the Kennet and Avon Canal, before crossing open fields and heading back past thatched cottages to Kintbury. The walk starts by the 12th-century St Mary's church in Kintbury, where in early spring you can see carpets of snowdrops. The chequer-work tower was added in the 15th century. Folk tales say that the original tower was destroyed in a storm and the great bell fell into the river. However, the locals were prevented in their attempts to retrieve it by the Kintbury Witch! There are always colourful narrowboats drifting by as you walk along the canal – and keep your crusts from the picnic handy to feed the swans and ducks.

Getting there Kintbury is south of the A4, between Hungerford and Newbury. From Station Road, turn into High Street, then go right into Church Street to reach The Croft on the left. There is a train station in Kintbury, which is close to the Dundas Arms and point 2 of the walk.

Length of walk 2½ miles.
Time 2 hours.
Terrain Towpath, public footpaths and roads make this gentle walk suitable for all-terrain pushchairs. There is a short section of country road with no pavements.
Start/Parking At the roadside at The Croft, in front of St Mary's church (GR: SU 384670).
Map OS Explorer 158 Newbury & Hungerford.
Refreshments There are benches dotted along the first stretch of the towpath where you can eat a picnic, or further on by Shepherd's Bridge a grassy bank is a peaceful spot. The Prince of Wales in Newbury Street, towards the end of the walk, has a beer garden, serves food and welcomes children and dogs.

The Walk

❶ Follow the public footpath sign at the corner of St Mary's church and walk diagonally across the churchyard, passing a First World

◆ Fun Things to See and Do ◆

See if you can **spot the following** as you walk: a cockerel high up in the sky, a dovecote, two tree houses, two Second World War pillboxes, a no fishing sign, a male and female mallard and a swan.

As you walk past St Mary's church, you can see a **sundial** next to the church clock. Stop and check whether both clocks are telling the same time. There are Roman numerals around the edge of the sundial. The sun shines on the triangular pointer called a gnomon (pronounced *no-men*). This casts a shadow on the appropriate hour line to show the time. A sundial is the oldest way of telling the time; as far back as 5,000 BC people used the shadow from a gnomon to show the time of day.

War memorial on your right. Follow a bricked path with a couple of small steps and pass the impressive gates of The Old Vicarage on your left. Then cross the bridge in front of you over the Kennet and Avon Canal. At the end of the bridge turn right down to the towpath.

2 Walk along the towpath with the canal on your right. Go through the gate and cross the road with care, go through another gate and continue along the towpath, passing the Dundas Arms on the other side of the canal. Cross a footbridge over a weir and continue straight on. This is a very peaceful stretch of the route, with views to the right across the fields that you will walk across later. You soon see Shepherd's Bridge ahead of you, an ideal spot for a picnic.

3 Cross the bridge to a public footpath sign giving you a choice of routes. The path on your left heads up to Irish Hill, but to return to Kintbury, take the path on your right and walk diagonally across the field, being careful of the farmer's crops on either side

Watching the narrowboats from the bridge

of the path. You can see the canal over on your right as you walk. Head for an obvious gap in the hedge and go through the next field to another gap in the hedge. In early summer these fields are filled with the sound of skylarks, while birds of prey hover in the sky above you. The footpath leads to a tarmac farm track. Go straight on, heading west with the hedge on your right and the rooftops at the edge of Kintbury ahead of you. Pass by the side of a metal farm gate to the road.

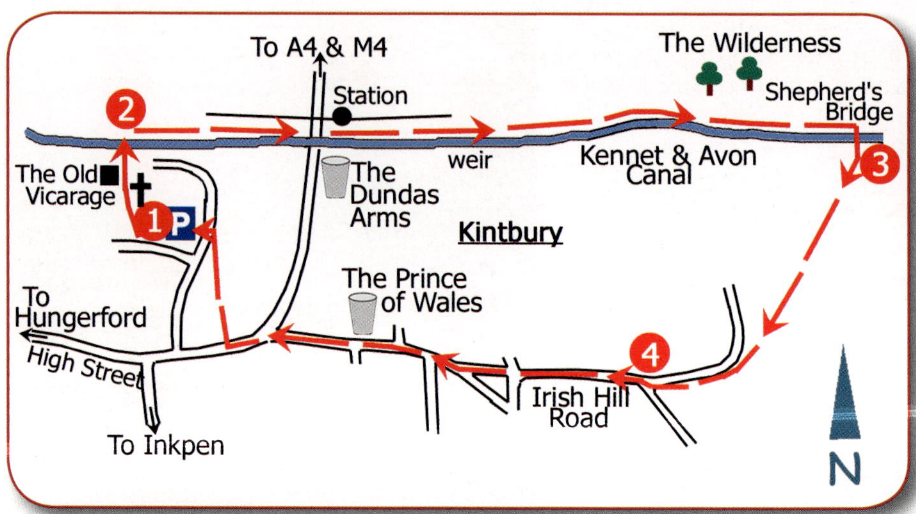

4 This stretch of road is very quiet, but there is no pavement, so walk with care straight on. Pass a village sign for Kintbury and the sign for Kintbury Park Farm on your right. At the end of the road, cross Holt Road and turn right. Cross Burtons Hill and continue straight on down the hill into Kintbury. Pass the Prince of Wales pub on your right and at the end of the road, cross the road in front of you and turn left. At the edge of the allotments turn right onto a public footpath along the edge of these small, well-tended plots – see which vegetables the children can spot growing there. At the end of the allotments turn left and go through an ancient wooden turnstile. The church is on your left.

◆ Background Notes ◆

The **Kennet and Avon Canal** links the River Thames at Reading with the River Avon at Bristol. It was opened in stages between 1723 and 1820 but through neglect in the 20th century became unnavigable. However, after a restoration campaign the canal was reopened by HM The Queen in 1990 and now the towpath is used by walkers and cyclists while holidaymakers can watch the scenery pass by from the deck of a colourful narrowboat.

Donnington Castle
Treading in the Soldiers' Footsteps

Racing to be 'king of the castle' at Donnington

This is a ramble packed with interest. Children will love playing in the ruins of medieval Donnington Castle, where this walks starts and finishes. Its grassy banks are perfect for running up and down and the remaining walls and gatehouse stand as an impressive reminder of the destruction of the English Civil War. From this vantage point, you also get stunning views across the Lambourn Valley. The walk follows the Lambourn Valley Way through Castle Wood to the picturesque village of Bagnor, before heading along a shady tunnel of native woodland to the edge of Snelsmore Common Country Park. The common is a designated Site of Special Scientific Interest and is packed with wildlife. The infamous Newbury bypass runs through the southern edge of the common and during the protests in the 1990s, this was the focal area for the protestors' tree camps and tunnels. However, now the woodland trees are home to the great spotted woodpecker, nuthatch and tawny owl, while wild ponies graze on the heathland.

Kiddiwalks in Berkshire

3

Length of walk 3 miles.
Time 2 hours.
Terrain Easy walking on footpaths and bridleways. Welly boots advisable after wet weather as there may be some muddy patches. A shorter walk to Bagnor then back again to Donnington would be suitable for all-terrain pushchairs and younger families.
Start/Parking Free parking at Donnington Castle car park (GR: SU 462692).
Map OS Explorer 158 Newbury & Hungerford.
Refreshments The Blackbird pub at Bagnor has a pretty beer garden with a children's play area and plenty of picnic tables. Donnington Castle is also an ideal spot for a picnic. If you walk further into Snelsmore Country Park, there is a large picnic area by the car park, with permanent barbecues that you can use.

The Walk

1 With your back to the car park and the castle in front of you, take the public footpath sign to the left of the car park. Follow the path straight on, past blackberry bushes and mixed woodland with views up to Donnington Castle on your right. This path is part of the Lambourn Valley Way and leads you through Castle Wood. At the end of the woodland, take the left footpath, which skirts the edge of the golf course, down to a turning on the right. Cross the bridge over the busy Newbury bypass. Turn left at the end of the bridge and follow a tarmacked path past newly-planted trees. There are plaques on the left naming the local schools that helped to plant them.

2 The path ends at a kissing gate and some houses at the edge of Bagnor village. Turn right and follow the gravel path to the picnic tables for the Blackbird pub. Pass the pub on your right and walk down the main street. Take care as, although it is a quiet road, there are no pavements here. There is a footpath sign just before the bridge. Turn right here and follow the grassy path between two houses. The house on the right has an impressive dovecote fixed to its wall.

3 Go through a kissing gate and continue gently uphill with open fields either side of you. There is a small bench at the top of this path, where you can stop and admire the views back over the Lambourn Valley. Then go through a kissing gate into a small copse. Turn left and follow the shady path, past oak, beech and holly trees. The tunnel of trees and hedgerows you are walking through gradually turns into Ashpiece Copse, and the edge of Snelsmore Common.

The picnic area at Snelsmore Common is a popular spot for ball games and barbecues

4 Just before a wooden fence, there is a green footpath sign with a kissing gate on your right. Go through the gate and follow the

◆ Fun Things to See and Do ◆

The ruins and earthworks of **Donnington Castle** are filled with adventure. Children can imagine what it would have been like when medieval lords and ladies lived in the castle. In the wall of the gatehouse you can still see the fireplaces. The square holes are where the wooden posts supporting the floor would have been. Walk round the gatehouse and see how many gargoyles you can spot (see *Background Notes* for the answer). Gargoyles are water spouts, built to keep the rain water off the surface of the walls. No one knows for certain why they were carved into such fantastical creatures – maybe it was believed that gargoyles would protect the building and the people inside it from evil spirits.

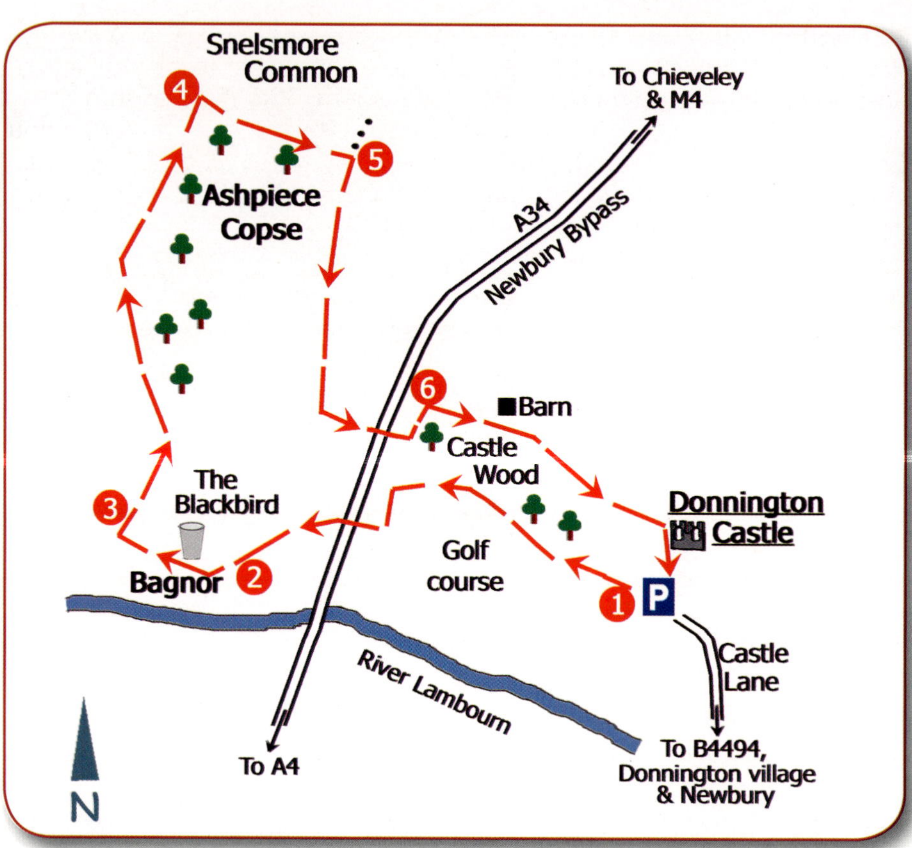

path through the woods, keeping the wire fence on your left. This is a very pretty stretch of the walk as the path winds gradually upwards through the woods to another kissing gate. Go through the gate to leave the woods behind you. Follow the grassy track straight on to a public bridleway.

5 Turn right and continue over open, high ground with fields on the left and the golf course on your right. The bridleway turns into a tarmacked track and you can see the bypass ahead of you. Follow the path as it takes you down to a footpath over the bypass. As you cross, you can see the bridge you crossed earlier in the walk, on your right.

6 Continue straight on, up a short, steep slope. Turn right and pass a very dilapidated barn on your left, with Donnington Castle looming on the horizon directly in front of you. Continue straight on to a farm gate and walk towards the castle. A swing gate on the right leads you into the earthworks surrounding Donnington Castle and when you are ready to leave, a path heads down the steep slope to the car park.

◆ Background Notes ◆

There is an English Heritage display board by the car park, which gives a brief history of the 14th-century **Donnington Castle** and its role during the English Civil War. The star-shaped earthworks surrounding the castle were dug by the Royalists, under the orders of John Boys, when they seized the castle from its Parliamentarian owners after the **First Battle of Newbury** in September 1643. The Royalists held out against a Parliamentary siege in July 1644, when King Charles I marched to their rescue. However, after the indecisive **Second Battle of Newbury** in October 1644, John Boys and his Royalist garrison were forced to valiantly hold the castle again, this time against a gruelling 18-month siege, before eventually surrendering and being allowed to march out of the castle alive. In 1646 Parliament voted to demolish the castle, leaving just the four-towered gatehouse proudly standing on top of the hill.

The protests to stop the nine miles of the **Newbury Bypass** from being built in the 1990s were so fierce that they have been dubbed the **Third Battle of Newbury**. Added to the £100 million cost of the road, £24 million was spent on extra security to protect the contractors from the attempts by the protestors to stop their work. As you stand on the footbridge, with four lanes of traffic constantly roaring beneath you, the need for this bypass might seem inescapable. However, the road runs through three Sites of Special Scientific Interest and caused 120 acres of woodland to be cleared, as well as the felling of 10,000 mature trees. This area was also home to the rare Desmoulin's whorl snail. The snails were moved from Rack Marsh in Bagnor to a new site, but are now extinct locally.

There are 15 surviving **gargoyles** at Donnington Castle.

West Ilsley

Racehorse Country

This walk takes you through the delightful village of West Ilsley and up onto the Berkshire Downs. There are fantastic views across this sweeping landscape, which is an Area of Outstanding Natural Beauty. The downland is also famous for being racehorse country and horse lovers will enjoy peeping over the gates of the immaculate Keeper's Stables and admiring the racehorses in the fields. Other much smaller but no less alluring inhabitants of the downland are the butterflies. In high summer, the wildflowers either side of your path are covered with a variety of butterflies, including the beautiful and rare chalkhill blue.

Getting there West Ilsley lies 2 miles west of the A34, to the north of Newbury and the M4. The village is clearly signed from the A34. Drive through the village along Main Street, passing the cricket ground on your left. Then as the road bends to the left, veer onto the track on your right to park.

Length of walk 2 miles.
Time About 2 hours, depending on how long you spend admiring the racehorses!
Terrain This is an easy walk along pavements, gravel tracks and grassy paths. There are some gentle uphill stretches.
Start/Parking Free off-road car parking at the start of the track off Main Street (GR: SU 471825).
Map OS Explorer 170 Abingdon, Wantage & Vale of White Horse.

Refreshments The historic Harrow pub in West Ilsley has the perfect location for an outdoor lunch. It is raised up from the road and is directly opposite the cricket pitch and village pond. You can choose between the picnic tables at Cricket View Garden or Pond View Garden. The pub is full of character, serves food at lunchtimes and welcomes children.

The Walk

1 From the parking spot, walk back along Main Street, heading towards East Ilsley, passing the Harrow on your left. Pass All Saints' church on your right, with its beautiful lychgate, then near a first-floor bay window that sticks out over the pavement, cross the road with care and take the gravel path signed 'Church Way'. Follow the path between the houses to a lane. Walk straight

◆ Fun Things to See and Do ◆

Next to the cricket ground in West Ilsley is a great **adventure playground** where children can practise their swinging and climbing skills while you keep an eye on the cricket. See if your children can read the score from the large scoreboard and how many wickets and overs there are.

4

P
To Farnborough
Main Street
The Harrow
Cricket ground
West Ilsley
Church Way
To A34
Keeper's Stables
West Ilsley Stables
The wildflowers attract lots of butterflies
1
2
3
N

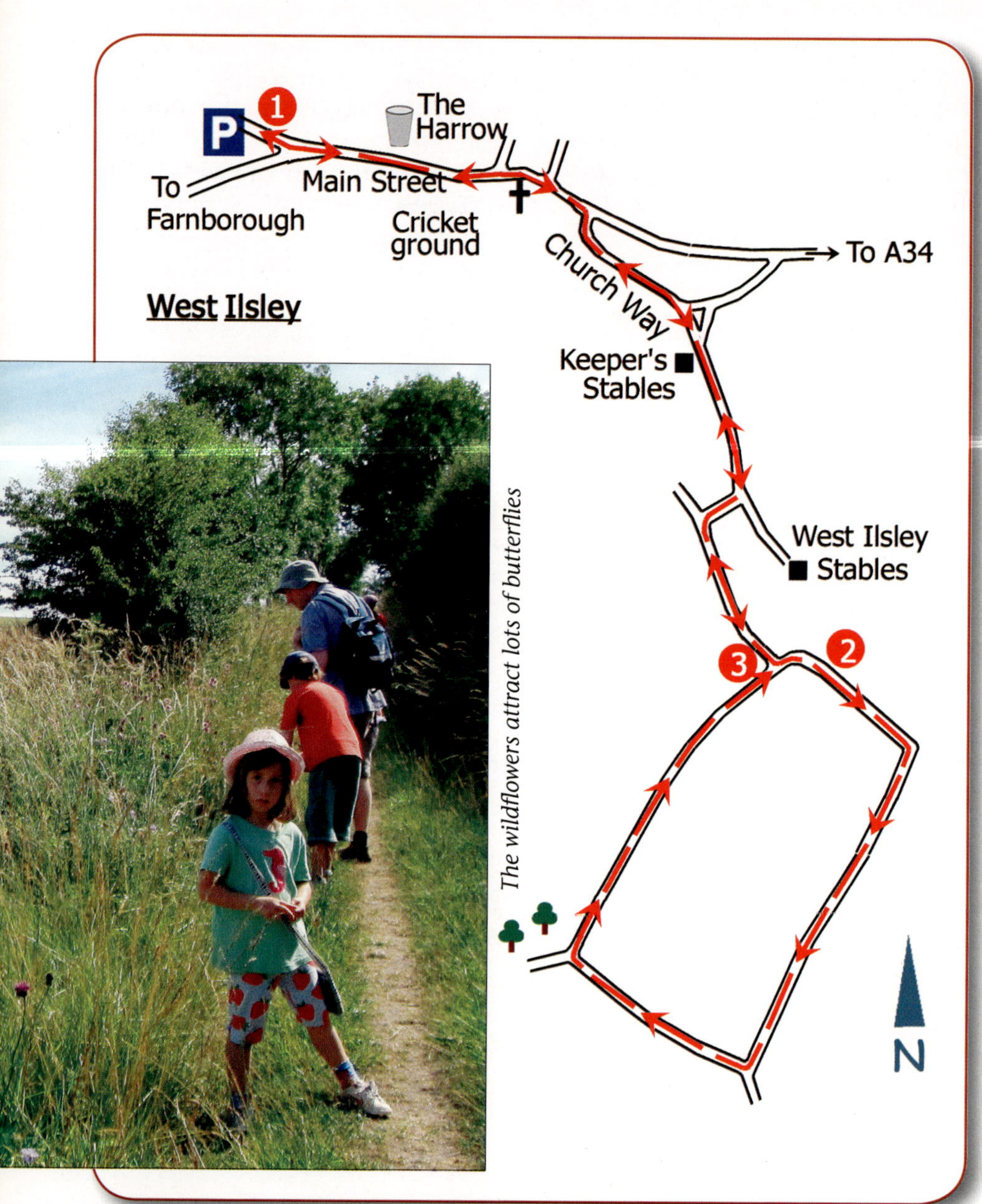

ahead, passing Keeper's Stables on your right. This is signed as a public bridleway but you do get the occasional car, so walk along the wide grassy verge. Just before West Ilsley Stables and a private property sign, turn right following the public bridleway and walk a short distance up to a T-junction. There are racehorse gallops in front of you, that are also a popular nesting ground for skylarks. Turn left and follow the path to the edge of the field. You come to a path going uphill on your right, which you will come down later in the walk. But for now turn left, following the public bridleway for a couple of yards, then take the uphill path on your right.

2 This is a lovely path, edged with wildflowers in season, that leads up to the downs. The views at the top are spectacular, and it's a brilliant spot to look out for birds of prey hovering in the open skies around you. At the top of the path turn right and head south along the path. The path gradually leads downwards to a junction of paths, where you turn right and follow the public bridleway between two fences. At the end of this path turn right onto a public footpath. You will shortly see the village of West Ilsley in the valley on your left.

3 When you get to the bottom, turn left to retrace your steps. Turn right at the blue arrow to lead back to the road. Then turn left and walk to the gravel byway that leads you back to Main Street. Turn left and walk back to your car.

◆ Background Notes ◆

You can be in no doubt that you are walking on **chalk downland** on a dry summer's day as clouds of white dust are kicked up with each step. This area has been inhabited by man since prehistoric times. Britain's oldest road, the Ridgeway, passes a mile away from the village, and has been used by travellers for at least 5,000 years. If your children are wondering why they are walking UP to the DOWNS, you could tell them that the word comes from the Anglo-Saxon *dun*, which means *hill*. And over time an area with lots of *duns* became known as *downland*. This chalk soil isn't suitable for crops, but it is ideal for **racehorses** as the springy turf protects their legs from injury.

Hampstead Norreys

A Minibug Safari

A minibug safari in a wildflower meadow

This shady walk takes you through ancient woodland filled with adventure. At the start of the walk you pass the remains of a Norman motte and bailey castle; the wooden castle has rotted away over time leaving just the large earth mound. Children will love running up its slopes to look out for the approaching enemy! There are many footpaths through the woods, with 'Walkers Welcome' signs to help you, so if anyone gets tired it is easy to find a short cut back. In late summer this is an ideal spot for blackberry picking.

Length of walk 1¼ miles.
Time 1½ hours. Take a little more time to look around the churchyard and play in Dean Meadow.
Terrain Well-defined woodland paths and bridleways, although you should be prepared for muddy patches after wet weather. Not suitable for pushchairs.
Start/Parking At the roadside by the iron railings in front of The Manor House or in front of St Mary's church (GR: SU 529763).

Getting there Taking the B4009 from Newbury, drive through Hermitage into Hampstead Norreys. Turn right at a small roundabout onto Church Street, following the brown tourist sign to The Living Rainforest. Look out for the black iron railings on your right by the church from where the walk starts.

Map OS Explorer 158 Newbury & Hungerford.
Refreshments The White Hart inn further down from the church has a large beer garden with picnic tables and a children's play area.

The Walk

1 Follow the public footpath sign at the corner of St Mary's churchyard. This is a beautiful church complete with ancient yew trees, gothic headstones and noisy crows to add to the atmosphere. A heritage sign in the churchyard records the village's entry in the Domesday Book of 1086. The path comes out opposite Dean Meadow and the children's play area.

2 Turn left and follow the bridleway signs past an information sign about the motte and a small cemetery on your right. You will see the woods in front of you. Follow the public footpath

◆ Fun Things to See and Do ◆

You pass **Dean Meadow** near the start and end of the walk. This is a good spot to stop for a picnic as there is a children's play area with swings, slides and seesaws, as well as a couple of benches for the adults.

There is a large wildflower meadow in the middle of the walk. Challenge your children to a **minibug safari** and see what they can find remembering to just look and not disturb the insects. As you walk through the grass in late summer listen out for the male grasshoppers trying to impress the female grasshoppers. They make their distinctive noise by rubbing their leg against their wing to cause a vibration.

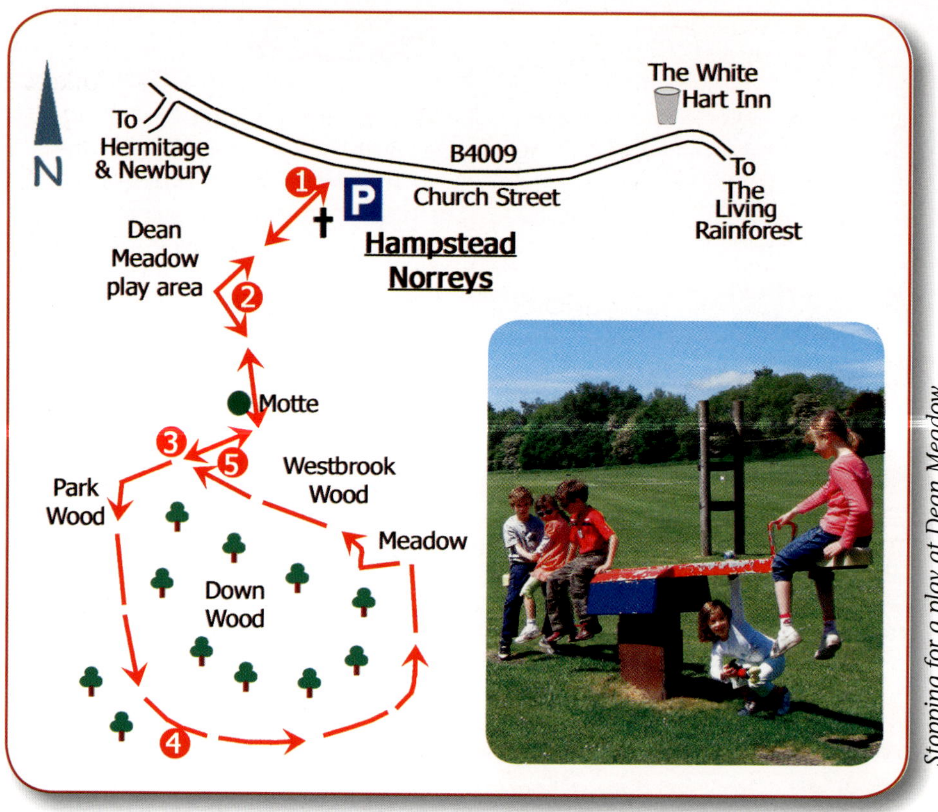

Stopping for a play at Dean Meadow

sign that leads you gently upwards into Park Wood. Shortly you will find a junction of footpaths; take the central path straight through the wood. You will see the motte through the trees on your right. Take the path on the right, just past the sign for the motte, and follow the path upwards.

3 Pass a bridleway on your left with 'Walkers Welcome' signs on your left and right, and continue straight on. The path levels out; pass a bridleway path on your left and continue straight on to the edge of the woods, where the path veers left. As you walk, you pass newly planted trees on your right and blackberry bushes on either side of the path. Continue straight on this path, ignoring a path to your left, until the path is crossed by a wide grassy track.

Take the path ahead of you that leads back into the woods. Continue straight ahead until eventually you see a farm field through the trees and the edge of the wood.

4 Turn left to the field then follow the farm track left, with the field on your right, passing 'Walkers Welcome' signs. The track veers left and takes you away from the field and back into the woods. Continue on this path, ignoring paths to your left and right. Continue straight on to pass some newly-planted oak and beech trees on your right. Eventually, the path comes out into an area of open ground, filled with wildflowers in early summer. Take the path immediately to your left that leads back into the woods. Continue until you reach a junction of paths where you turn right, following the 'Walkers Welcome' sign downhill along a wide path. There may still be a large fallen tree on the right here – perfect for climbing along. In the winter, you can see the River Pang snaking its way through the edge of the woods on your right. Continue ahead as the path veers left. Walk through the woods until you come to point 3 of the walk, with the motte down on your right.

5 Turn right and retrace your steps back down the path, turning left at the motte and walk out of the woods. Then go back down the path to the footpath sign at the edge of St Mary's churchyard.

◆ Background Notes ◆

The stream that you see in the village and by the edge of the woods is the start of the **River Pang**. Its source lies a few miles north of Hampstead Norreys, near the village of Compton. It runs for about 14 miles, eventually joining the mighty River Thames at Pangbourne.

The Living Rainforest on the northern edge of Hampstead Norreys has two large glasshouses filled with tropical plants while birds and butterflies fly freely around you. There are also monkeys, turtles, tortoises and a very sleepy crocodile to look at. To find out about any special events and entry fees, visit www.livingrainforest.org or telephone 01635 202444.

Yattendon

Where Christmas Trees Grow

Yattendon lies in the heart of the North Wessex Downs, an Area of Outstanding Natural Beauty. This peaceful walk starts in one of the prettiest villages in West Berkshire, with half-timbered cottages, a village square and a collection of Best Kept Village awards proudly displayed on various walls. The Yattendon Estate, which owns the surrounding land, has left wide margins and hedgerows between the fields; these are good for walkers, as well as wildlife. In May, the copses are carpeted with bluebells, while the open skies above the fields are filled with the song of skylarks, as well as the occasional bird of prey. This walk takes you to the edge of the hamlet of Ashampstead before returning across the fields.

Getting there Heading from Newbury, take the B4009 towards Hermitage. Turn right in Hermitage onto the Yattendon road and follow the signs into the village.

Length of walk 4 miles.
Time 3 hours, longer if you visit the farm shop.
Terrain Grassy field paths and farm tracks. There are a few stiles to climb over and a very short stretch of country road with no pavement.

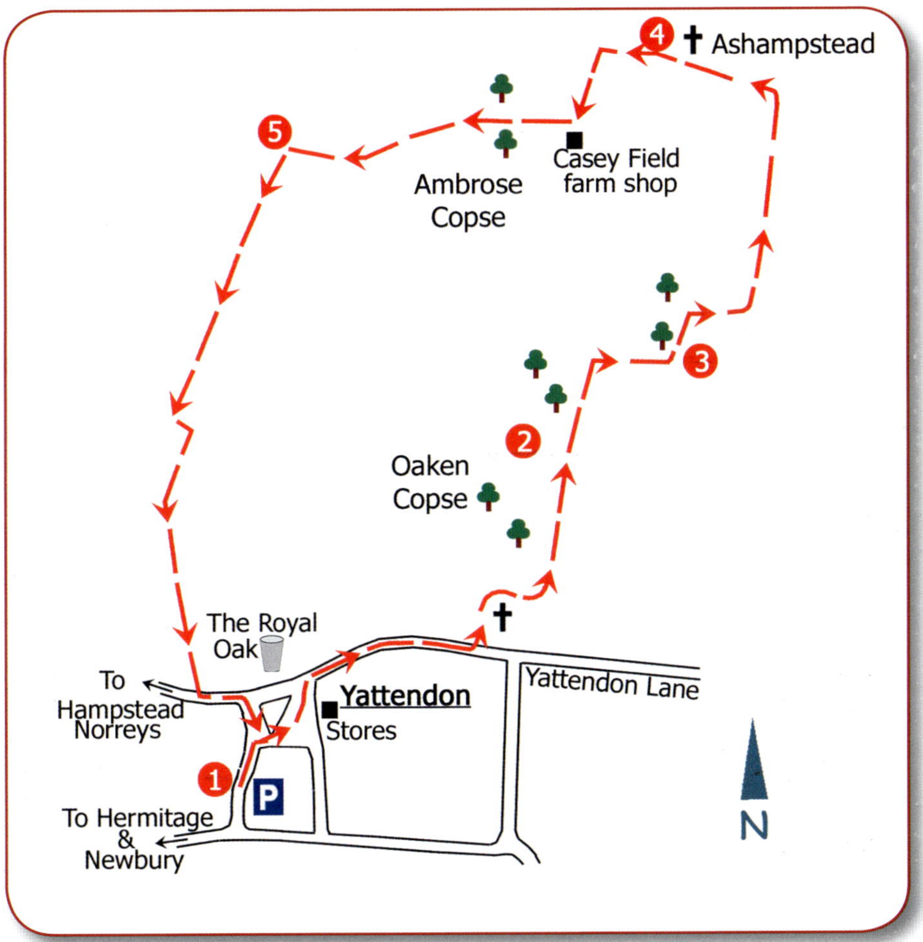

Kiddiwalks in Berkshire

Start/Parking There is a free car park on the right as you enter the village from the Hermitage direction (GR: SU 554745).
Map OS Explorer 158 Newbury & Hungerford.
Refreshments The Royal Oak has a pretty walled beer garden, or you could sit and watch village life at one of the tables in front of the pub.

The Walk

1 Turn right from the car park and walk across the village square and past the butcher's shop, heading towards the church. The public footpath sign is at the edge of the churchyard. Turn left and follow the path as it skirts the edge of the churchyard. It then turns left to head away from the village, passing a copse then open fields.

2 You come to a crossroads of footpaths with an ancient oak tree on your left. Cross the farm track, ignoring the paths left and right and go straight on, following the public footpath with a copse on your left. Follow the footpath round the field for about a mile

Children will love seeing the lambs

◆ Fun Things to See and Do ◆

In Yattendon, see if you can **spot the following**: a crown, a brass horse's head and a green telephone box.

As you walk across the farmland, **look out for** fields of Christmas trees – Yattendon Estate has around one million trees at various stages of growth. The cattle are Friesian Holsteins and there is a rare pedigree herd of British White cattle. In summer, if you are very lucky you might see the endangered stone-curlew. It is the size of a crow, with yellow legs, yellow eyes and a yellow and black beak. Also look out for a large, reddish bird of prey with a forked tail. This is the rare, red kite, which has been saved from national extinction and is now thriving in Berkshire. Younger children will enjoy seeing the lambs in spring and picking blackberries from the hedgerows in autumn.

and you will come to a wooden post with a public footpath sign on your left leading into the woods.

3 Go straight on then through the gap in the fence in front of you to a farm track surrounded by arable fields. Turn to the right and follow the path towards the footpath sign that you can see ahead of you. This sign tells you that you have walked 1½ miles from Yattendon. Turn left, following the 'Restricted Byway' sign, through a shady tunnel of mixed hedgerow and cow parsley. Pass a footpath sign on your right and continue straight on.

The path turns into a small road at the edge of Ashampstead, with two chocolate-box cottages on your left. Follow the road round to the left for a short distance, heading towards St Clement's church. There is a large yew tree at the edge of the churchyard by a public footpath sign. Go through the gate and walk through the churchyard to a swing gate.

4 Cross a small grassy area, then go through another swing gate into a large arable field. The farmer has carefully left the footpath clear and it is easy to follow the path straight in front of you across the field. Go through a swing gate out of the field onto a concrete track and turn left. There is a 10 mph speed limit but take care as, although it is a bridleway, cars do pass you, heading for the farm shop at the end of the track. Just before the entrance to the shop, a public bridleway sign on your right leads into Ambrose Copse. Watch out for pheasants scurrying across your path as you walk through the woods. At the end of the path turn right and follow the public bridleway path through a ribbon of native trees between the fields. You come out of the trees to a choice of tracks and a footpath sign.

5 Turn left, following the yellow footpath sign south across the field; again the farmer has left a clear path for walkers to follow. There is a large oak tree in the middle of the field. At the edge of the field, follow the public footpath sign in front of you into a small spinney. Cross the stile, then another stile, following the public footpath signs into a large field. Walk along the edge of the field to another stile, then cross a tarmac farm track to another stile with a public footpath sign. Follow this wide grassy path with a hawthorn hedge on your right to a stile at the other end leading to another field. At the end of the field follow the footpath sign left to the stile. Cross the stile and turn left, following the edge of an arable field for a short distance. At the edge of the field turn right, with a hedge on your left, heading towards a small metal farm shed. Before you reach the shed, you will see a footpath sign on your left. Cut diagonally across the field, passing a farmhouse, and head down to the road. Then turn left and walk carefully along the side of the road into Yattendon. The car park is on your right.

◆ Background Notes ◆

Yattendon has held a **May Day fête** since medieval times. It now takes place every year on the Whitsun Bank Holiday. The magnificent tithe barn is filled with craft and cake stalls, or you could try your luck at the local sport of Christmas tree throwing!

Bucklebury Common

A Woodland Adventure

An oak climbing frame on Bucklebury Common

The village of Upper Bucklebury is not only blessed with a wonderfully whimsical name, but it is also surrounded by ancient, wooded commonland. This walk explores Bucklebury Common to the west of the village. These native woods are filled with adventure, crisscrossed with paths to explore, as well as open glades to run through and an unexpected area of open heathland.

Length of walk 2 miles.
Time 2 hours.
Terrain Easy walking along
woodland paths and bridleways.
The bridleways can get very
muddy after wet weather, so wear
wellies or be prepared to hop
around the puddles.
Start/Parking There is a small
free car park immediately on the
left as you drive into Briff Lane
(GR: SU 537688).
Map OS Explorer 158 Newbury &
Hungerford. Pack a compass as well
to check you are walking in the
right direction through the woods.
Refreshments The Cottage Inn
in Upper Bucklebury serves food.
It has a fenced front garden with

picnic benches. Alternatively, the
grassy area behind the pond at
The Slade is a good picnic spot.

The Walk

1 Follow the red byway sign at
the right edge of the car park into
the woods, heading north. Pass
under some power cables then
take the left fork of the path in
front of you through the woods.
Follow the red byway sign straight
on. Your path crosses another
path, but continue straight on,
passing another narrower path.
Shortly you come to a wider
track crossing your route, where
you turn left. To check you have
come to the right track, look for
a post at the end of the path on
your right. This track leads you to
Bucklebury Quiet Lane.

2 Cross the lane and follow the
'Public Bridleway' sign across
the road and through the woods.
Pass under power cables, then
see blue bridleway signs on your
right and continue straight on,
heading west. The path crosses a
tarmacked road with a bridleway
sign on your left. Go over the road
and follow the path through the
woods. Ignore a right turn that
leads back the way you came, and
continue for a short distance until
you come to a post on your right.

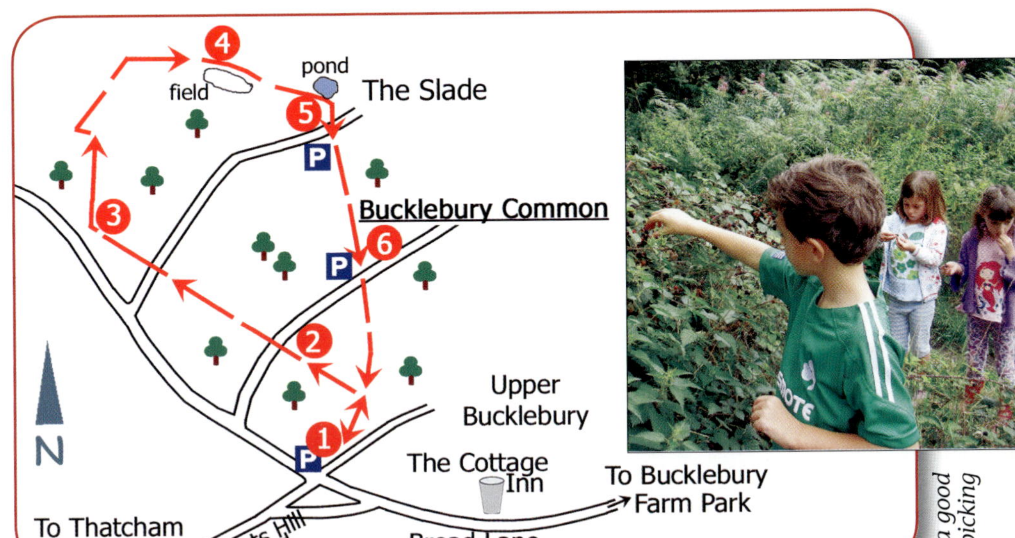

The start of the walk is a good spot for blackberry picking

3 Turn right and follow the blue bridleway sign north, passing a blue arrow on your left. This path ends at a slight clearing with lots of routes going in different directions. Turn left heading towards a sunken area of ground that is always filled with water, then immediately right by this water to head downhill on a rutted path. When you come to a path crossing your route, turn right and follow this path, heading east. Pass an ancient oak tree in a slight clearing that has had generations of initials scratched into its bark. Continue straight on and then head right at a fork.

◆ Fun Things to See and Do ◆

There are lots of **oak trees to climb** as you walk through the woods. Horse lovers will enjoy watching the horses trotting by on the many bridleways that crisscross the common. See if you can spot **hoof and deer prints** in the wet mud of the bridleways. In autumn, the woods are filled with different kinds of **mushrooms and toadstools**.

4 Pass a grassy field on your right, edged with oak trees. There is a large black water container here leading to a tin bath for horses to drink from. Continue along the path; gradually the trees thin out and the path leads to a grassy area. Walk towards a small pond with a house on your right. There is a crocodile here lurking in the water. This is the edge of The Slade.

5 There is a yellow public footpath sign on a telegraph pole next to the house. Follow this narrow footpath past houses and gardens to a small country road. On your left is Slade Cottage. Cross the road with care and opposite the cottage is a small gravel car park and a map of the Bucklebury Estate. The footpath is to the left of the map and leads through the woods. Follow the yellow footpath signs and cross a wooden footbridge over a narrow stream, then head gently uphill. There is a series of logs laid out across the path to help walkers across the boggy ground. Pass a yellow footpath arrow and follow the higher left path into an area of heathland with heather and gorse. Follow the narrow path through the gorse, heading south, passing a yellow footpath sign on your right, until you come to a gravel car park.

6 Cross the tarmac road and follow the public bridleway sign straight on and into the woods. The path passes below some power cables. Take the right fork in the path, and cross the wide track that you walked along in point 1. Go straight on to retrace your steps, passing red byway arrows on your right, and follow the path back under the power cables. Take the right fork in the path and walk back to the car park.

◆ Background Notes ◆

Follow the road through Upper Bucklebury to visit **Bucklebury Farm Park**. It is open from early spring until late autumn and has all the usual children's farm attractions surrounded by beautiful countryside. The entrance fee includes a tractor and trailer ride through the deer park and a chance to hand-feed the herd. There is a café selling ice creams and hot and cold snacks. Check the website (www.buckleburyfarmpark.co.uk) for opening times and prices or telephone 0118 971 4002.

Thatcham Lakes

Water Birds and Reedbeds

On the towpath

Pack a bird guidebook for this walk as Thatcham Lakes and the surrounding reedbeds are filled with water birds. This walk takes you through the nature reserve to a pretty stretch of water by the Kennet and Avon Canal, before returning to Thatcham Lake and the Discovery Centre. This is definitely a walk for wellies, not only because a wetlands landscape is inevitably going to be muddy in places, but also as there is a perfect spot for splashing around by the water – where the pebbly bank meets the shallow water by the eastern edge of the lake.

Getting there From the A4, take the turning at the traffic lights directly opposite the West Berkshire Community Hospital, onto Lower Way. Continue past green metal fences to a track on your right, signed 'Thatcham Nature Discovery Centre'. Follow the signs to the car park.

Length of walk 2¼ miles.
Time 2 hours.
Terrain Towpaths, gravel paths, boardwalks and earth tracks make this walk suitable for all-terrain pushchairs; however, the footpath crosses the railway tracks at one point, so you would have to be able to carry the pushchair over this short distance.
Start/Parking Free car parking at Thatcham Nature Discovery Centre (GR: SU 507672).

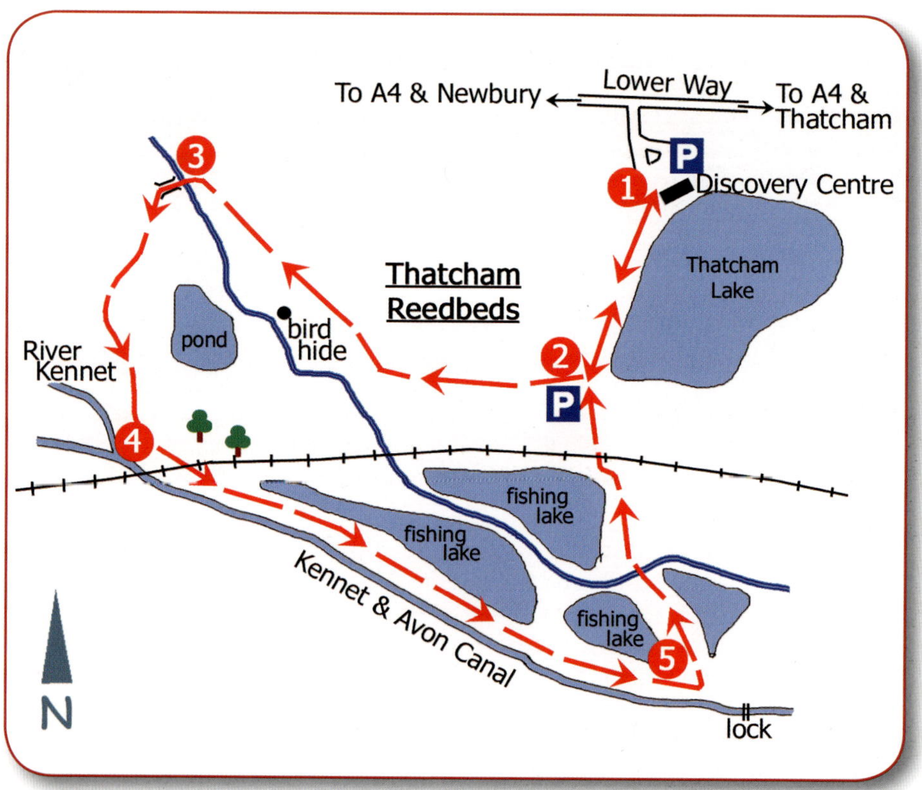

Map OS Explorer 158 Newbury & Hungerford.

Refreshments The Discovery Centre has a café selling soup, sandwiches, ice creams and excellent cakes. Alternatively, bring a picnic and sit at one of the picnic tables or benches dotted round the lake.

The Walk

1 From the car park, pass the two adventure playgrounds and walk to the right of the Discovery Centre. Then follow the gravel path straight ahead, with the lake on your left. Younger families could follow this gentle path round Thatcham Lake and back to the Discovery Centre. However, to do the full walk, when the path bends left round the top of the lake, go through the green metal fence and cross diagonally to the public footpath sign.

2 Take the right path, passing a

◆ Fun Things to See and Do ◆

Thatcham Nature Discovery Centre is free to visit. It has two adventure playgrounds; the one for younger children has various creatures carved into the apparatus. Inside the Centre, there are hands-on exhibitions for children to explore and find out about the wildlife and habitat around them. A webcam positioned on the island in the middle of the lake is linked to a screen inside the Centre, where you can watch the nesting birds. The Centre sells bags of special food to **feed the many ducks and Canada geese** that are always waiting expectantly outside.

See how many different types of **water birds you can spot** on the walk. There are moorhens, coots, herons, mallards, great crested grebes, mute swans, Canada geese and tufted ducks. In the summer, swallows and sand martins swoop through the sky while birds of prey hover over the water.

small car parking area on your left. Soon you will see reedbeds on your left and a thicket of trees and hedgerow on your right. At a metal sign, take the grassy path straight ahead of you; ignore the path on the left that leads under the railway bridge. This winding path has blackthorn, or May blossom, and hawthorn on your right with small ponds and reedbeds on your left. Cross a short metal bridge and go straight on. There is a green metal fence on your right now and you pass a fenced boardwalk leading to a bird hide on your left. Continue along the main path until you see an information board.

3 Turn left and cross a small bridge. The path meanders through tall reedbeds with large, open skies above you. Try and spot some of the many birds you can hear singing all around. Boardwalks along various parts of the walk help you in the boggier areas.

4 As you come out of the reedbeds, the path leads up to the banks of the River Kennet, at the point where it joins the Kennet and Avon Canal. Turn left and walk along the bank and under the railway bridge. Although you can't see the tracks, at this point of the walk you are close to the railway lines and occasionally the odd train might whistle past. Pass a Second World War pillbox on your left, built to defend this strategic spot in case of a German invasion. The ponds on your left become wider now as you walk through the nature reserve.

5 When you see the lock gates ahead, look out for a wooden gate down on your left. Go through the gate and follow a hedged path that leads you away from the canal and through the fishing lakes. Look out for herons, who also appreciate the fine fishing opportunities here. Cross a metal bridge; you will be able to see the railway tracks in front of you. There are more reedbeds on your right as the path leads up to a metal kissing gate and the train tracks. Cross the tracks with great care and go through the metal gate on the other side of the tracks to continue along the footpath. This path leads back to point 2 of the walk. There is a bench at the corner of the lake where you can stop and watch the ducks, before either following the path you took at the start of the walk straight back to the Discovery Centre, or turning right to walk round Thatcham Lake and back to the car park.

◆ Background Notes ◆

This area is now a **Site of Special Scientific Interest** and a **Special Area of Conservation**. The wetlands landscape is a haven for a range of breeding birds, as well as moths, butterflies and the rare Desmoulin's whorl snail. However, although flint tools dating back 10,000 years to the Mesolithic period have been found in the peat beds, many of the lakes, including Thatcham Lake, date back only as far as the late 1970s. This area was used for gravel extraction – you can still see signs of ongoing works on the walk – and it wasn't landscaped until the mid 1980s. The Discovery Centre, opened in 1995, has been extended and the newly improved centre opened in July 2007. Unfortunately, this was the very day that torrential rain caused massive flooding in the area, causing the Centre to have to close again for a period, to repair the damage.

Bowdown Woods Nature Reserve, Newbury

If You Go Down to the Woods Today ...

Get set for a woodland adventure

Bowdown Woods Nature Reserve is a hidden gem on the edge of Newbury. There are three woods on the site, Bowdown, Bomb Site and Baynes. This peaceful woodland is managed by the Wildlife Trust, which has provided information boards for visitors, as well as clearly marked 'Wildlife Walks' to guide you round the site. In spring the woods are carpeted with bluebells and the scent from the flowers fills the air, while in late summer the slopes are resplendent with a mantle of purple heather and yellow gorse. At all times of the year the woods are magical and packed with wildlife.

Bowdown Woods Nature Reserve, Newbury

Getting there Bowdown Woods are 2½ miles south-east of Newbury. Head east from Greenham towards Thatcham along Bury's Bank Road, cross a cattle grid then take the signed turning on your left along a bumpy track to reach the car park.

Length of walk 1½ miles, or ¾ mile for the Bomb Site walk.
Time 1 hour.
Terrain The path is easy to walk but there are some steep areas that make it unsuitable for pushchairs. The surfaced track around the Bomb Site is perfect for pushchairs or after rainy weather, when the lower slopes in Bowdown Wood can get muddy.
Start/Parking Start from the free Bomb Site car park (GR: SU 504655).

Map OS Explorer 158 Newbury & Hungerford.
Refreshments There are lots of family-friendly restaurants and cafés in Newbury.

The Walk

1 Go through the gate at the left of the car park, where there is a large information board and map of the area. This is the Bomb Site. Walk straight ahead along a surfaced track, ignoring a path off to your right. You shortly come to a permissive path on your left, which leads you steeply down and then up again, with wonderful views to your right across the Kennet Valley and Bowdown House on your left. Alternatively, you could continue straight along the main track for a shorter ¾ mile walk round the Bomb Site. This circular path comes out just beyond the information board.

◆ Fun Things to See and Do ◆

Roe deer are called 'Fairies of the Woods' because they are hard to spot and very shy, but you might be lucky as there are lots of deer in Bowdown Wood. Look out for their prints in the mud; their cloven hooves leave a mark that looks like two slots. Their coats are foxy red in the summer and greyish brown in the winter, although all you might see is the white patch on their rump as they run away!

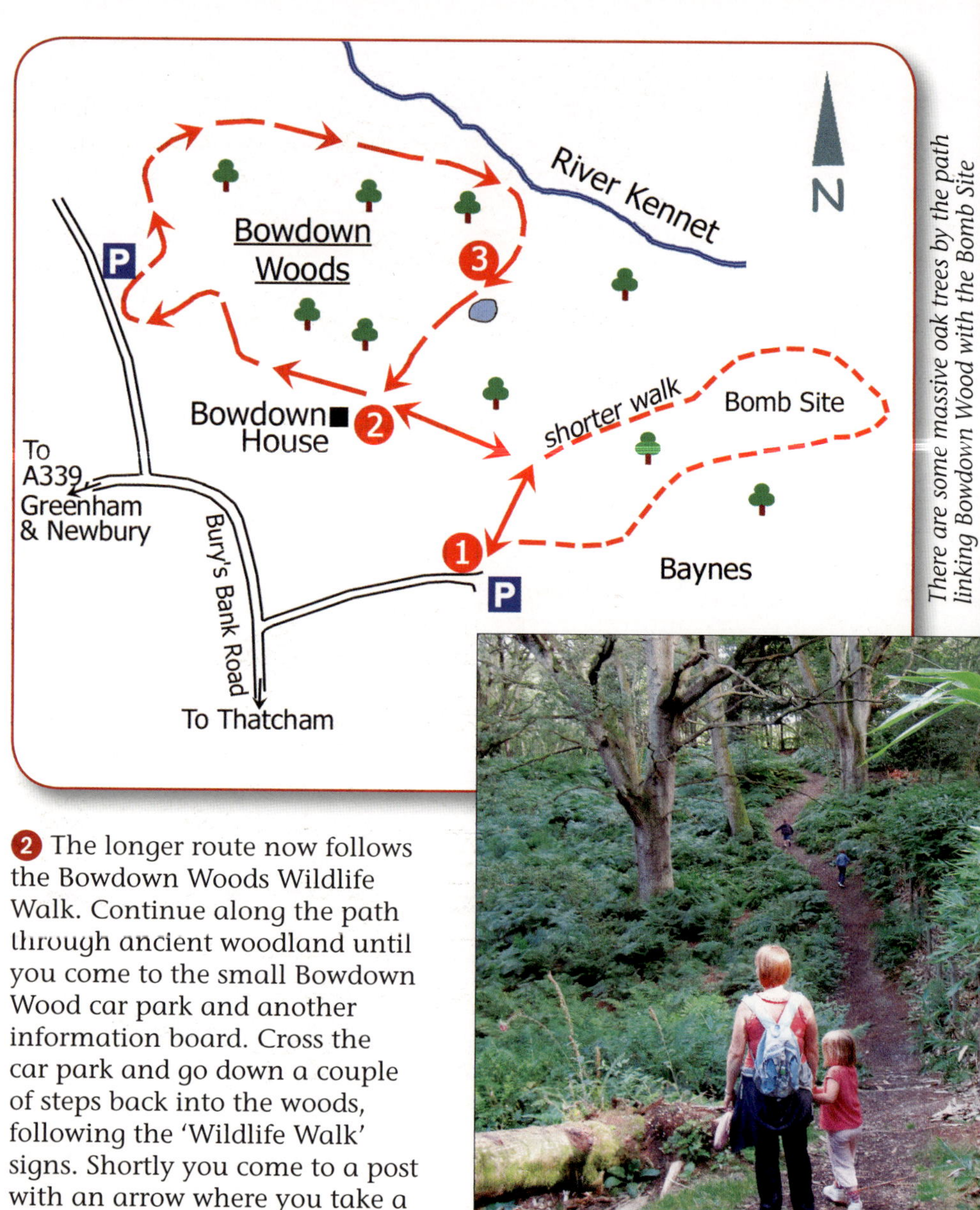

There are some massive oak trees by the path linking Bowdown Wood with the Bomb Site

2 The longer route now follows the Bowdown Woods Wildlife Walk. Continue along the path through ancient woodland until you come to the small Bowdown Wood car park and another information board. Cross the car park and go down a couple of steps back into the woods, following the 'Wildlife Walk' signs. Shortly you come to a post with an arrow where you take a left turn downhill. At the end of the path veer right, to skirt the edge of the woods. Continue on, passing a sign on your left for the Wildlife Walk.

3 The path winds its way through the woods until leading you back uphill. Watch out for a small pond on your left, which is filled with newts and frogs. It is also a good spot to stop and watch the dragonflies in summer. At the top of the path you will recognise the route from earlier in the walk and see Bowdown House in front of you. Turn left to retrace your steps. When you get to the top of the slope, turn right to the car park, or if you are still feeling adventurous, left to follow the circular path round the Bomb Site.

◆ Background Notes ◆

Berkshire, Buckinghamshire and Oxfordshire Wildlife Trust and West Berkshire Council are creating a **Living Landscape** linking Bowdown Woods Nature Reserve and the heathland at Greenham Common, with the River Kennet and Thatcham Reedbeds. The idea is to create an uninterrupted space for wildlife to travel between these different habitats. **Bowdown House**, built in 1911 in the Arts and Crafts style, was the home of King Haakon VII of Norway from 1940 until 1942, after the Norwegian royal family escaped from the Nazi invasion of Norway in 1940. The house is now a residential conference centre.

Greenham Common, on the other side of Bury's Bank Road, is a Site of Special Scientific Interest and home to many rare ground-nesting birds. However, its past has been much less peaceful. The RAF acquired the common in 1941. It was initially home to RAF trainer units, then USAAF Fighter Groups and Troop Carrier Groups used the common as a base. During the Cold War in the 1950s, the Americans developed the area for their post-war jet bombers and in the 1980s Greenham Common became the first site in the UK to store fully operational cruise missiles. The Greenham Common Women's Peace Camp protested against these nuclear weapons throughout the 1980s. However, the missiles stayed until 1991 and the MoD finally closed the base in 1993.

Pangbourne

Walking the Thames Path

This walk starts by Whitchurch toll bridge and follows a timeless stretch of the Thames Path through Pangbourne Meadow. This area of water meadows is owned by the National Trust and is filled with wildflowers and butterflies in summer. Kenneth Grahame wrote *The Wind in the Willows* while he was living in Cookham, but it was the Thames at Pangbourne that was the inspiration for E.H. Shepard's evocative illustrations. The peace of the river is only disturbed by the occasional leisure boat or rowing team to watch, as well as the ubiquitous Thames swans drifting majestically by.

Getting there From the A4, follow the A340 into Pangbourne. Turn right onto High Street then left onto the B471, Whitchurch Road. Just before you go over the toll bridge, the car park is on your right. Pangbourne rail station is in the west of the town, near the river.

Length of walk 1½ miles.
Time 1½ hours.
Terrain Flat field paths and pavements. Suitable for all-terrain pushchairs.
Start/Parking The River Meadow pay and display car park is free on Sundays and bank holidays (GR: SU 637768). If the car park is full, continue straight on over the Whitchurch toll bridge – it costs 40p each way – and park roadside in Whitchurch, near the Greyhound pub.

Map OS Explorer 159 Reading.
Refreshments There are lots of pubs and cafés in Pangbourne. Alternatively, bring a picnic and find a spot by the Thames.

The Walk

1 Take the gravel footpath out of the car park to the recreation ground on your left. Walk across the grass to the River Thames, then follow the Thames Path. Pass a National Trust sign on your left for Pangbourne Meadow. In summer, the meadow is filled with wildflowers. Then cross a wooden footbridge, following the sign for Thames Path National Trail. This field path leads you slightly away from the river, through a wildflower meadow. Walk between two horizontal posts then straight ahead for about 50 yards to cross a concrete footbridge with a gate.

2 Go through the gate and turn right. Walk through the field to

◆ Fun Things to See and Do ◆

The walk starts at a riverside recreation park that is an ideal spot for **picnics** and **ball games**. Younger children will enjoy spending time in the middle of the walk in the **children's play area**. The Thames is full of life with **various boats to look at**. If you bring a pair of binoculars, children can read the boats' names as they pass by.

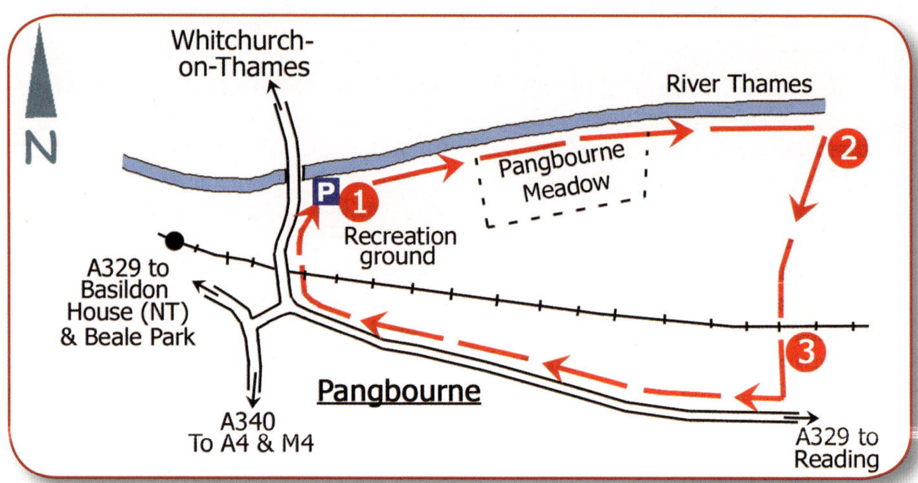

a kissing gate by the side of an iron farm gate. Then continue straight on with fields either side of you. Pass a small sewage works on your right then go through a metal kissing gate. Follow the path left, under a railway bridge, then it veers to the right until shortly you come to a public footpath sign on your left, leading you across the field. But directly ahead of you, you will see a children's play area, so you could stop for a while here,

The Thames Path is a perfect spot on a sunny day

then back track to continue your walk.

3 At the public footpath sign, go through a metal kissing gate and follow the path with a field on your left. At the end of the path you come to a sign telling you that it is ½ mile to the Thames.

The busy road in front of you is the A329. Turn right and walk along the pavement back into Pangbourne. Turn right at the George Hotel and walk under the bridge and back to the car park on your right, or spend some time exploring the shops and cafés in Pangbourne.

◆ Background Notes ◆

The **Thames Path National Trail** runs for 184 miles from the river's source in the Cotswolds to London, and is England's most recent national trail. Walking the whole path would lead you past Oxford's dreaming spires and Berkshire's water meadows, through historic Windsor and Hampton to the Thames Barrier in the heart of London. The Romans established Londinium around AD 50, recognising the importance of the River Thames for trade. In medieval times, Cotswold wool was brought down the River Thames to London and by the 18th century London was the world's busiest port. The river only ceased to be an important trading route in the second half of the 20th century. Now leisure boats rather than barges make their way down the Thames and London's historic docklands have been regenerated into an expensive residential and commercial centre, with the towering Canary Wharf business district at its steely centre.

Beale Park Wildlife Park and Gardens, on the western edge of Pangbourne, is open from March to October. There are lots of animals, a small pets area and deer park, as well as various play areas to suit different age groups. If your children are tired from the walk, you could hop on the narrow-gauge steam and diesel railway for a one-mile trip round the park, or if you are feeling more extravagant take a river cruise. **Thames Rivercruise** offers a half-hour round cruise from Beale Park. The Beale Park website (www.bealepark.co.uk) gives opening times and prices for the park and river cruise or telephone 0844 826 1761.

11

Moor Copse Nature Reserve, Tidmarsh
A Walk on the Wild Side

Walking through the bluebells in Park Wood

This varied walk takes you through three different wildlife habitats. It starts by the banks of the beautiful River Pang. Look out for trout swimming through the clear water, while in summer metallic blue and green damselflies hover by the riverside. The path then heads through coppiced native woodland filled with flowers and birdsong before returning beside wildflower meadows. In early May, the bluebells in Park Wood are spectacular. Information boards positioned along the walk help you to identify the birds and insects that you can see and hear all around you.

Getting there Leave the A4 just west of Theale and take the A340 heading north towards Pangbourne. Immediately after the M4 bridge look out for the right turn down to the car park. It is not signed at the roadside.

Length of walk 1½ miles.
Time 1½ hours, longer if you stop for a picnic.
Terrain Easy walking along woodland paths and grassy fields, although the fields get boggy after rain. The woods are suitable for all-terrain pushchairs and there are plenty of footpath signs if younger families want a shorter walk.
Start/Parking Free parking at the Wildlife Trust car park (GR: SU 635738).
Map OS Explorer 159 Reading.
Refreshments The Greyhound in nearby Tidmarsh is a beautiful thatched pub and there is a children's play area across the road. It has a large restaurant area and welcomes children.

The Walk

1 From the car park turn right onto the tarmac track then take the immediate left turn through the wooden fence into Hogmoor Copse. Follow the boardwalk in front of you to the banks of the River Pang. The footpath follows the river as it snakes through the woodland. Look out for the Wildlife Trust sign on the left showing *Life on the River Pang*. Continue along the path, keeping the clear waters of the Pang on your right. If you are lucky, you might spot deer grazing in the fields on the other side of the river. Pass a very decrepit footbridge on your right, and just after this another footbridge, which you cross. Ignore the path to the left and go straight ahead, leaving the river behind you, and through the gate into Park Wood.

2 In early May this area is carpeted with bluebells. Just before the information board *Letting the Sun In*, turn right following the 'Wildlife Walk' sign through Hodsall Ride. There are lots of bird boxes in these woods so be careful to stay on the paths and keep dogs on a lead so as not to disturb the wildlife. The path takes you through woods filled with wildflowers and birdsong. As you reach the edge of the woods, there is a sign explaining *Coppicing* on your left and a left turn. To shorten the walk, you could turn left here, then

Kiddiwalks in Berkshire

◆ Fun Things to See and Do ◆

Berks, Bucks and Oxon Wildlife Trust has placed excellent **nature information boards** along the way, with pictures and captions telling you about the insects, birds and animals that live here, as well as showing how the landscape is cared for to encourage wildlife to thrive. **See if you can find answers** to the following wildlife questions as you walk: Can a grass snake swim? Where does a demoiselle lay her eggs? What does a tawny owl like for his dinner? Who thinks a black slug is delicious? Find the answers on the information boards, or look at the end of *Background Notes*.

For younger children, the footbridge over the River Pang is the perfect spot for **Pooh sticks** and as you walk through the woods there are plenty of log pile houses to spot, but hopefully no Gruffalo! There are thick leaves to rustle in autumn and blackberries to pick in late summer.

It's eat or be eaten for the wildlife at Moor Copse

left again to return to Hogmoor Copse. But to continue the walk, follow the 'Parish Walk' signpost straight on and out of the woods through a kissing gate.

3 Cross straight over 5-Acre Field to a gate and another information board about wildlife at the *Edge of the Wood*. Go through the metal gate and

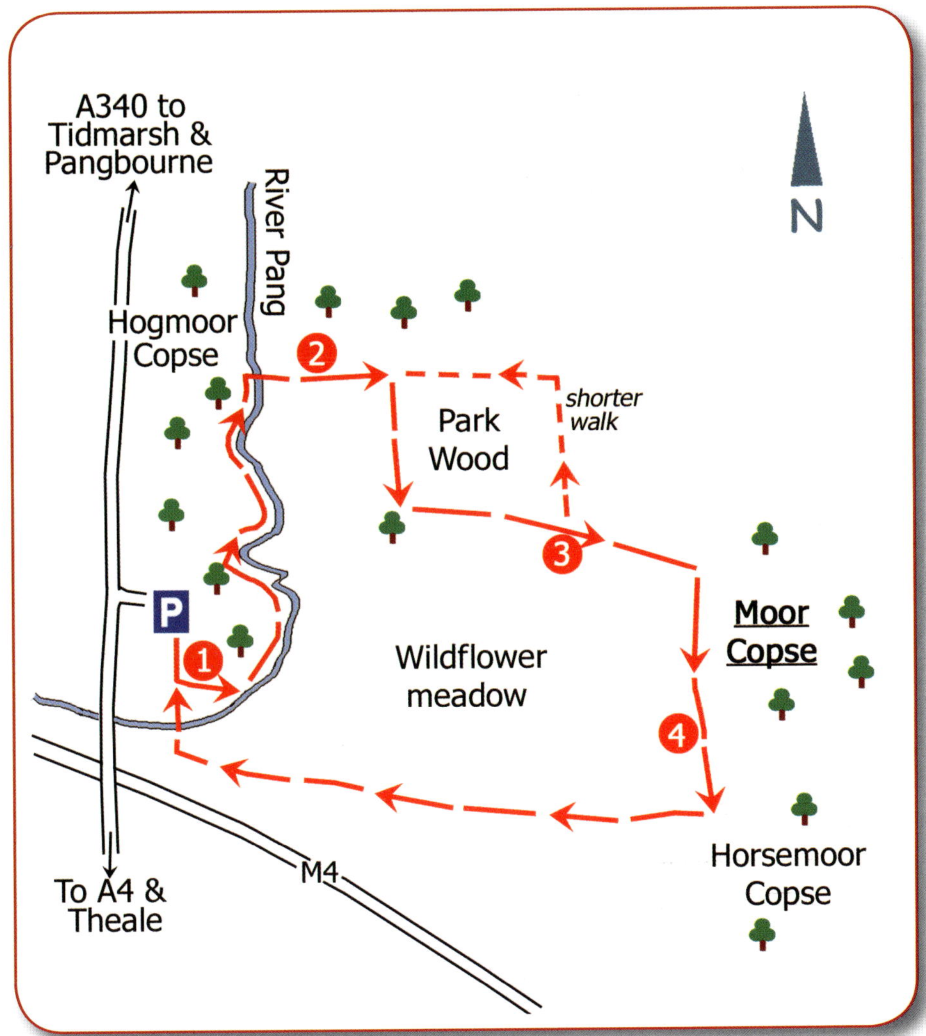

follow the path through the hazel coppice. Pass a *Coppicing in Woodland* sign on your left. These woods are home to all three types of British woodpecker, so listen out for their distinctive hammering sound as they guard their territories. Cross a small bridge over a stream and walk through Baker's Ride.

4 Pass some log piles on your right and go through a metal gate into open fields, heading south, with the trees of Horsemoor Copse in front of you. Cross the field, then through a gate and over a boardwalk bridge. Do not go through the gate on your left into the woods, but turn right and head across the fields and through two farm gates, keeping the wire fence on your right. The land on your right is a new conservation area where the Wildlife Trust is creating a wildflower meadow. Look out for the information sign *Restoring a Wildflower Meadow* on your right. Walk through a final gate, which takes you out of the fields to a track. Turn right and walk with blackberry bushes either side of the path. At the end of the path turn left and follow the path over the bridge and back to the car park.

◆ Background Notes ◆

This land once belonged to the architect Lewis E. Trevers OBE, who moved to the area in the 1930s. He managed the woods and named the rides after his friends; for example, Baker's Ride is named after Brian Baker, who worked for the local Naturalists' Trust. Lewis died in 1983, leaving the land to **Berkshire, Buckinghamshire and Oxfordshire Wildlife Trust** in his will. The Trust has slowly been able to increase the size of the reserve, acquiring Barton's Copse in 1988 and an extra 72 acres of meadowland in 2006, following a public appeal. The arable field in the middle of the site is part of this new land, which BBOWT is turning into a traditional wildflower meadow.

Answers: Yes, grass snakes are good swimmers. A demoiselle lays her eggs on plants in the river. A tawny owl eats the common shrew. The common shrew, badger, song thrush and common frog all find a black slug delicious.

Hosehill Lake Nature Reserve, Theale
Don't Forget the Binoculars!

A tranquil spot on a summer's day

This walk is lots of fun, it is impossible to get lost and the one mile circular path makes it achievable for even the youngest of walkers. There are always plenty of water birds to spot and the large information boards positioned around the lake are packed with information and photos of the wildlife in the area, which makes it easy to discover exactly what you are looking at. If you bring a pair of binoculars, there are benches dotted round the route where you can sit and watch the birds on the two islands in the lake.

12

Getting there The nature reserve lies just south of junction 12 of the M4 and the A4 at Theale. From the A4, turn down Station Road, crossing over the railway line and the River Kennet. When you come to the Fox and Hounds in Sheffield Bottom, you will see the gated entrance to the reserve opposite you.

Length of walk 1 mile.
Time 1 hour.
Terrain Flat grassy path. Suitable for all-terrain pushchairs.
Start/Parking The Fox and Hounds pub has a large car park directly opposite the entrance to the nature reserve. Check with the landlord before parking there, as a courtesy (GR: SU 648698). Alternatively, there is a small lay-by on the west side of the reserve.
Map OS Explorer 159 Reading.

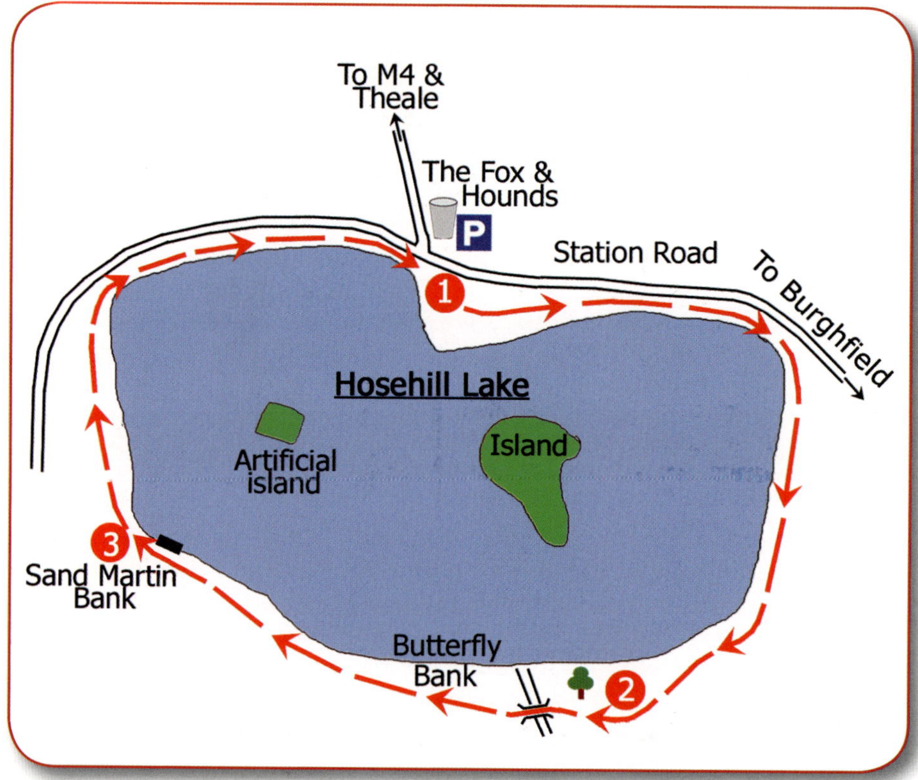

(Be careful as there is a mistake on the OS map, with Hosehill Lake marked as being further south in Wokefield Common. Ignore this and head for the pub symbol in Sheffield Bottom.) **Refreshments** The Fox and Hounds has a beer garden and a large menu, including a special children's menu. Alternatively, there are lots of beautifully carved benches dotted round the lake if you would rather have a picnic and watch the birds.

The Walk

1 Walk through the gate to the lake. Turn left to pass the information board and map, telling you about the area. Then follow the grassy path round the lake, passing a bird feeding station and viewing platform. The path veers to the right and goes through a wildflower meadow. In summer, this is a good spot to look for butterflies and dragonflies.

2 As you reach the southern edge of the lake the path leaves the side of the lake to take you through a small area of woodland called Copse Hill. Soon after crossing a footbridge, watch out for the butterfly bank. This is also a good spot to look at the birds on the main island in the lake.

◆ Fun Things to See and Do ◆

There are **birds and insects** to spot on a summer's day, while many water birds migrate to the lake in the winter. Information boards dotted around the lake help you to identify the birds and viewing platforms make it easy to look out across the reedbeds and lake. If your children want to **feed the ducks and waterfowl**, the best food is one that contains the nutrients, minerals and vitamins that birds need. Halved grapes, chopped lettuce, vegetables or fruit peels and defrosted garden peas or corn are much better for ducks than bread, and some of these items are food that you would have with you during a picnic anyway. Bread isn't a natural food for ducks and isn't very good for them; it is even worse for ducklings, who need to learn how to forage for natural foods that contain the nutrients they need.

3 Pass a bird feeding centre and the sand martin bank, before coming to a viewing spot and information board. Hosehill Lake is a popular spot for swallows and house and sand martins as they hawk for insects over the lake, their arrival marking the start of spring. The smaller artificial island was constructed to provide a nesting spot for common terns. The path continues round the lake to bring you back to the north side and the start of the walk.

There are lots of viewpoints for spotting birds on the islands

◆ Background Notes ◆

There has been a settlement at **Theale** since the Bronze Age, as the gravel terraces protected this area from the floodplain of the River Kennet. The water meadows at Theale were painted by the English Romantic painter **John Constable** (1776–1837). What was once a waterside village has grown into a busy town since the building of the M4 and houses now stand on these water meadows.

Hosehill Lake is one of many former **gravel pits** that are spread across the Theale floodplain. Gravel extraction grew in importance from the Middle Ages onwards as it was used for road building. It ended in the early 1980s and the open cast pits were filled with water to create one of Berkshire's most important birdwatching areas. Hosehill Lake has been a nature reserve since 1997.

Mortimer

Discovering a Roman Amphitheatre

The Roman amphitheatre is the perfect spot for a picnic and some gladiatorial combat

This walk takes you across fields to a brilliantly preserved Roman amphitheatre by the remains of the Roman town of Calleva Atrebatum. The amphitheatre is the perfect setting for children to indulge in some Roman role play. You could also continue into the site to see the Roman walls and the archaeologists at work. Horse lovers will enjoy the return journey as a green tunnel of ancient hedgerows leads you back past paddocks and a horse stud.

13

Getting there From Aldermaston on the A340, follow Welshman's Road into Mortimer. Turn right onto Victoria Road and look for the car park opposite the pub. From Junction 11 of the M4, head south down the A33. Turn right at the first roundabout. Pass Grazeley and follow the signs for about another 3 miles to Mortimer.

Length of walk 3½ miles.
Time 3 hours.
Terrain Fields, woodland paths and quiet country lanes. There is a short stretch of road on the way to the amphitheatre where there are no pavements, but the road is very quiet and you will hear a car coming long before it passes you.

Start/Parking There is a free car park in the centre of Mortimer directly opposite the Horse and Groom pub (GR: SU 657646).
Map OS Explorer 159 Reading.
Refreshments The Horse and Groom serves lunchtime meals and has a beer garden with a small gypsy caravan for children to play in. The route back passes the village store in Mortimer where you could get an ice cream to eat in the Fairground by the car park.

The Walk

1 From the car park turn left and walk a short distance down Victoria Road until you see a public footpath sign on the other side of the road. Cross the road with care and walk down a broad gravel driveway, then go left in front of the house down a narrow

◆ Fun Things to See and Do ◆

The **amphitheatre and town walls** are free to visit and open all year. During July and August, the University of Reading excavate the area between the walls. You can visit their site and see the archaeologists at work every day except Friday, between 10 am and 4.30 pm. Two raised walkways take you over the site with display boards to help you work out what you are looking at. There are also activity sheets for children and a dig pit and finds handling for future archaeologists to get their hands dirty! Admission and activities are free.

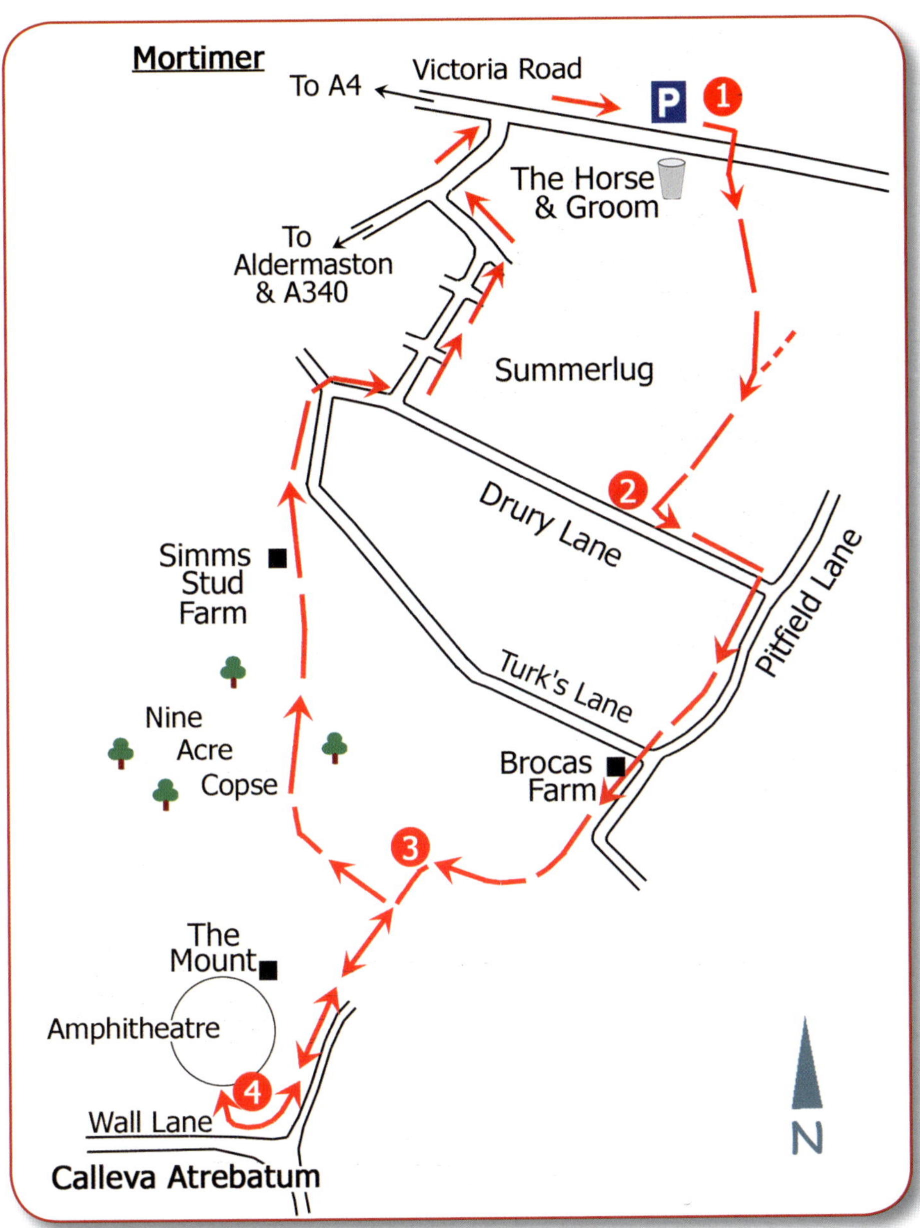

Mortimer
Victoria Road
To A4
P
1
The Horse & Groom
To Aldermaston & A340
Summerlug
2
Drury Lane
Simms Stud Farm
Pitfield Lane
Nine Acre Copse
Turk's Lane
Brocas Farm
3
The Mount
Amphitheatre
4
Wall Lane
Calleva Atrebatum
N

path to a field. Follow the edge of the field to the left, with the field on your right and gardens on your left. Pass a public footpath by a left turn and continue straight ahead, over a brook and into another field. The footpath runs directly ahead of you across the field, but to help the farmer's crops you could turn right and follow the field edge to the corner. Then go through the gap in the hedge to a country lane.

2 Turn left, passing a recreational route arrow. This lane has no pavements, so where possible walk along the grass verges. You pass a few houses on your right and at the end of the road turn right. Cross over a bridge, then pass Brocas Farm on your right and continue ahead. As the road veers left, go straight on and down a track, leaving the road behind, to walk with fields either side of you. At the corner of the field there is a yellow footpath arrow on a post. Walk along the edge of the field following a grassy path. The path veers right heading towards some electricity pylons, but before you reach the pylons turn left at a yellow footpath arrow and cross a stile.

A race across the fields to Mortimer

3 Walk straight ahead across the field to a small footbridge over a brook and another stile. Then walk directly across another field. Turn right out of the field and walk up to the road to a red post box. Turn right and go through the kissing gate to the amphitheatre.

4 When you have finished at the amphitheatre, walk back to the red post box. If you want to view the Roman walls, turn right along the road. To continue the walk, however, turn left at the postbox to retrace your steps. Go down the lane and at The Mount, turn to walk along the edge of the field. Veer left across the field to cross the two fields via stiles, as you did on the way here, passing under the pylons.

However, this time continue straight ahead across the field to a gap in the hedge, which leads you into Nine Acre Copse. Follow the path through these pretty woods. The path is edged with blackberry bushes so remember to bring a container with you in the autumn! Come out of the woods and across a short grassy path, then back into woods. You pass a blue bridleway sign and cross a small stream. Follow this path straight on and slightly uphill through a green tunnel of native hedgerow, with occasional glimpses of the fields on either side of you. On the left there are paddocks as you head towards Simms Stud Farm. Pass the farm on your left and continue to a lane, ignoring a footpath sign on your left. When you come to a junction turn left, with fields on your right and houses on your left. Then turn right down Drury lane. At a public footpath sign turn left down Summerlug. Follow the path straight on past a dead end sign on your left. Cross a road and continue ahead, passing another dead end sign on your left. At the end of this road turn left onto West End Road. Turn right to pass the village store and you will see the car park ahead of you on the other side of Victoria Road.

◆ Background Notes ◆

After the Roman invasion of Britain in AD 43, the existing Iron Age settlement of the Atrebates tribe developed into the Roman town of **Calleva Atrebatum**. The Romans left Britain at the beginning of the fifth century and by the sixth century this once thriving town had been abandoned. This is good news for archaeologists, as rather than having to dig through successive layers of building works, the site lay undisturbed until the late Victorian times. Between 1890 and 1909, the site between the walls was excavated by the Society of Antiquaries of London. They produced a complete plan of the Roman town by exposing the foundations of the stone buildings from between the second and fourth centuries AD. Unfortunately, as at the time they did not understand the archaeology of timber buildings, the earlier development of the town was lost. The site was then left alone until the 1970s when the Department of Archaeology at the University of Reading started excavations.

Loddon Nature Reserve, Twyford
Splashing in the Shallows

Splashing about by the side of the lake

This shady walk takes you around a lake that is home to many water birds. Willows spill over the path offering glimpses between their leaves of the islands in the middle of the lake. The second half of the walk follows the banks of the River Loddon, with water plants streaming just below the surface of the clear water. For most of the walk, although you are near a busy town, you can't see a single building. It is very easy to navigate and there are no roads in the nature reserve, so children can run ahead along the path and explore.

Loddon Nature Reserve, Twyford

Getting there Follow the A4 east out of Reading, go through Sonning then at the roundabout take the right turn onto the A3032 into Twyford. Continue straight on, following the signs for the car park, which is a right turn onto Polehampton Close. If you are coming by train, the reserve is a ½ mile walk westwards from Twyford station.

Length of walk 1½ miles.
Time About 1½ hours, longer if you stop for a picnic.
Terrain This is an easy walk on level paths with a few boardwalks through the nature reserve. It is unsurfaced so be prepared for muddy patches after wet weather.
Start/Parking There is a pay and display car park in Polehampton Close, Twyford (GR: SU 787758).
Map OS Explorer 159 Reading.
Refreshments There are benches dotted along the route where you can eat your picnic and watch the water birds on the lake. The Waggon and Horses public house has a large enclosed beer garden with a playhouse for children, as well as an impressive aviary.

The Walk

1 Turn left out of the car park and walk up to the main road. Turn left and walk over the railway bridge, heading out of town. Turn left by the Waggon and Horses public house and walk by the edge of its car park to a footbridge. This is a good spot for a game of Pooh sticks as the bridge crosses the gently flowing waters of Old River, a tributary of the River Loddon. Go through the gate into the nature reserve, there is an information board in front of you and a map.

2 Turn right and follow the shady path with the lake on your left. You can see the Old River through the trees on your right as it snakes through the nature reserve. Children can safely run ahead as there is no chance of getting lost along this path. The scrubby edges of the lake are home to lots of songbirds and in summer purple-loosestrife, yellow iris and orange balsam edge the path. As you reach the southern tip of the lake, you can see the railway bridge on your right. Follow the path round, keeping the lake on your left and the railway embankment on your right. Pass another nature reserve information sign and a small

14

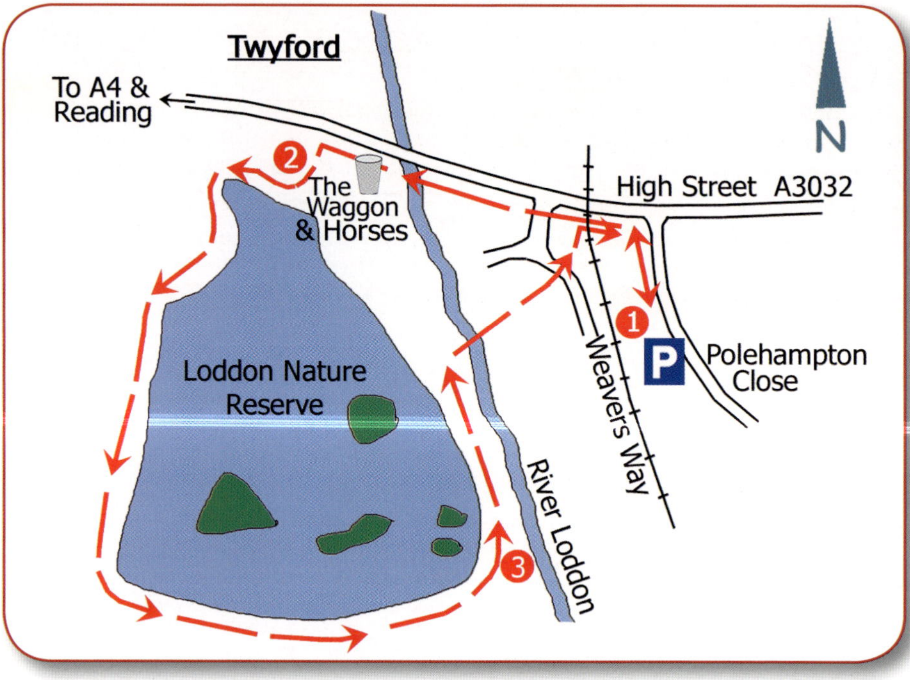

jetty. Continue along the path round the lake until you come to a public footpath sign on your right.

3 Now leave the lake and follow this short path to the banks of the River Loddon in front of you. There is an impressive arched

◆ Fun Things to See and Do ◆

Children should wear their wellies as the shallow edges of the lake are perfect for **paddling**. You can also look across to the island in the middle to glimpse the nesting birds. Bring a pair of binoculars and a bird book to see what you can spot. If your children want to **feed the birds**, look at the *Fun Things to See and Do* section in the Hosehill Lake Nature Reserve walk for some suggestions on what to give them.

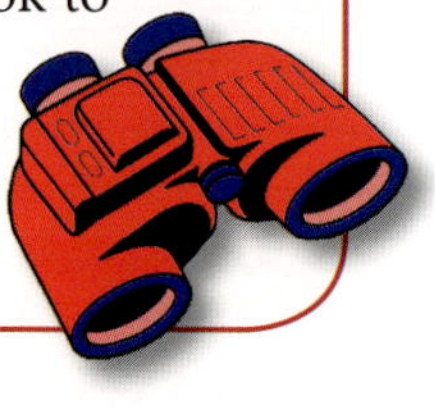

railway bridge on your right. Turn left and follow the footpath along the river bank. On your left the nettles are the perfect habitat for butterflies and dragonflies and there are views across the nature reserve to the lake. Ignore a footpath sign on your left, leading to a boardwalk and continue ahead to cross a narrow footpath over the river. Take care as the water is very fast here. Continue along the path past red brick flats on your left and cross another footbridge on your right. There is a measuring post here showing how deep the water is. Cross Weavers Way and follow the narrow gravel path in front of you to the main road. Turn right and walk back along the road, then turn right again to the car park.

Just one of the many lakeside picnic spots

◆ Background Notes ◆

Loddon Nature Reserve has been created from a flooded gravel pit next to the River Loddon. The small islands in the lake create perfect nesting grounds for common terns, lapwings and redshank, safe from predatory foxes. The willows and scrub that surround the lake are popular with nesting moorhens and coots, as well as butterflies and dragonflies. The reserve is owned and managed by Berkshire, Buckinghamshire and Oxfordshire Wildlife Trust, with the help of a local volunteer group who meet on occasional weekends to help with practical conservation. Look online at www.bbowt.org.uk to find out more about the Wildlife Trust and other nature reserves in Berkshire.

Finchampstead Ridges & the Blackwater Valley

Giant Trees and Water Birds

The walk starts by Wellingtonia Avenue, planted in 1869 to honour the general and statesman the Duke of Wellington (1769–1852). The impressive trees on either side of you are giant redwood, or Wellingtonia, as they were named in his honour. Giant redwoods aren't only massive, they are also very long-lived – sometimes for up to 3,000 years! After these towering trees, the native woodland on the next section of the walk might seem rather tame. Moor Green Lakes Nature Reserve takes you past lakes and water birds to the shady banks of the River Blackwater. After following a stretch of the Blackwater Valley Path, the return journey takes you past the western edge of the lakes to Finchampstead Ridges and an amazing view over three counties.

Finchampstead Ridges & the Blackwater Valley

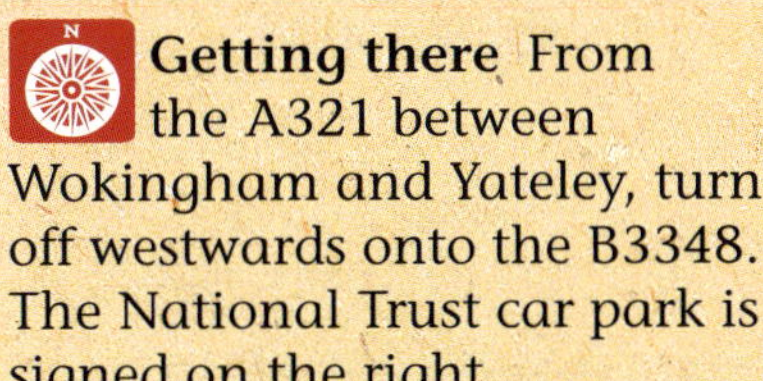

Getting there From the A321 between Wokingham and Yateley, turn off westwards onto the B3348. The National Trust car park is signed on the right.

Length of walk 3½ miles.
Time 3 hours.
Terrain The walk crosses fields, woodland paths and surfaced tracks. There are some stretches along country lanes where there are no pavements, so you will need to walk along the verge. There is an uphill stretch at the end.
Start/Parking Free parking at the National Trust Simons Wood car park (GR: SU 814638).
Map OS Explorer 159 Reading.
Refreshments The Greyhound in Finchampstead is a stylish pub with a large patio and garden.

Horseshoe Lake Activity Centre has lakeside picnic tables and barbecue facilities, although ask before using them, as a courtesy.

The Walk

1 From the car park, walk to the road and turn left down Wellingtonia Avenue. Walk along the pavement until you see a 'Restricted Byway' sign on your left and Barn End on your right. Cross the road with care and follow the track into the woods. Pass a public footpath sign on your right, and 100 yards later turn left, following the public footpath sign through the trees. The path leads through the woods to open fields. Over on your right you can see Beech Hill while Coalpit Copse on your left is carpeted with bluebells in May. The path veers left into the copse and the path becomes

◆ Fun Things to See and Do ◆

In the middle of the walk you pass **Horseshoe Lake Activity Centre**, which is a perfect place to stop for a rest. There is plenty of activity on the lake to watch, as the centre organises dinghy sailing, windsurfing, kayaking and canoeing. They also have a fantastic obstacle course that children are welcome to play on as long as you supervise them and they go on each section one at a time.

There are always boats and Canada geese to watch at Horseshoe Lake

kept watch from higher up the hill. Cross two more stiles through the meadows; this is farmland so dogs need to be on a lead. Cross the small road to follow the public footpath sign opposite, then go straight ahead through a kissing gate to follow the yellow arrow footpath sign.

3 You are now in Moor Green Lakes Nature Reserve and can see glimpses of a large lake on your right through the trees. Follow the path ahead of you and go through a kissing gate to pass Horseshoe Lake Activity Centre. Pass a car park on your left and a Blackwater Valley Path arrow. Turn right at the end of this track, to walk with the River Blackwater on your left and the lakes of the nature reserve on your right.

4 Just past an information sign on your right, take the public footpath on your right, following the yellow arrow. Continue straight on, then turn right, following the public footpath. There is a bridleway running alongside the path, on your left, and the lake on your right. Pass a bird hide and a bird feeding station. At the end of this path, go through a gate into a car park. Walk through the car park and turn right, to walk by the side of

wider. There are some large rhododendron shrubs here that are beautiful in June when covered in purple flowers.

2 The path comes out on a road to Ambarrow Farm. Turn left to follow the road. There is no pavement here so walk with care and keep to the green verge at the side of the road. Just before a left bend in the road, there is a public footpath sign on your right. Follow this path, with a small brook on your right. Go through a kissing gate into a field. Cross a stile into the next field. I walked through here in June and the field was filled with meadow buttercups, while a flock of geese

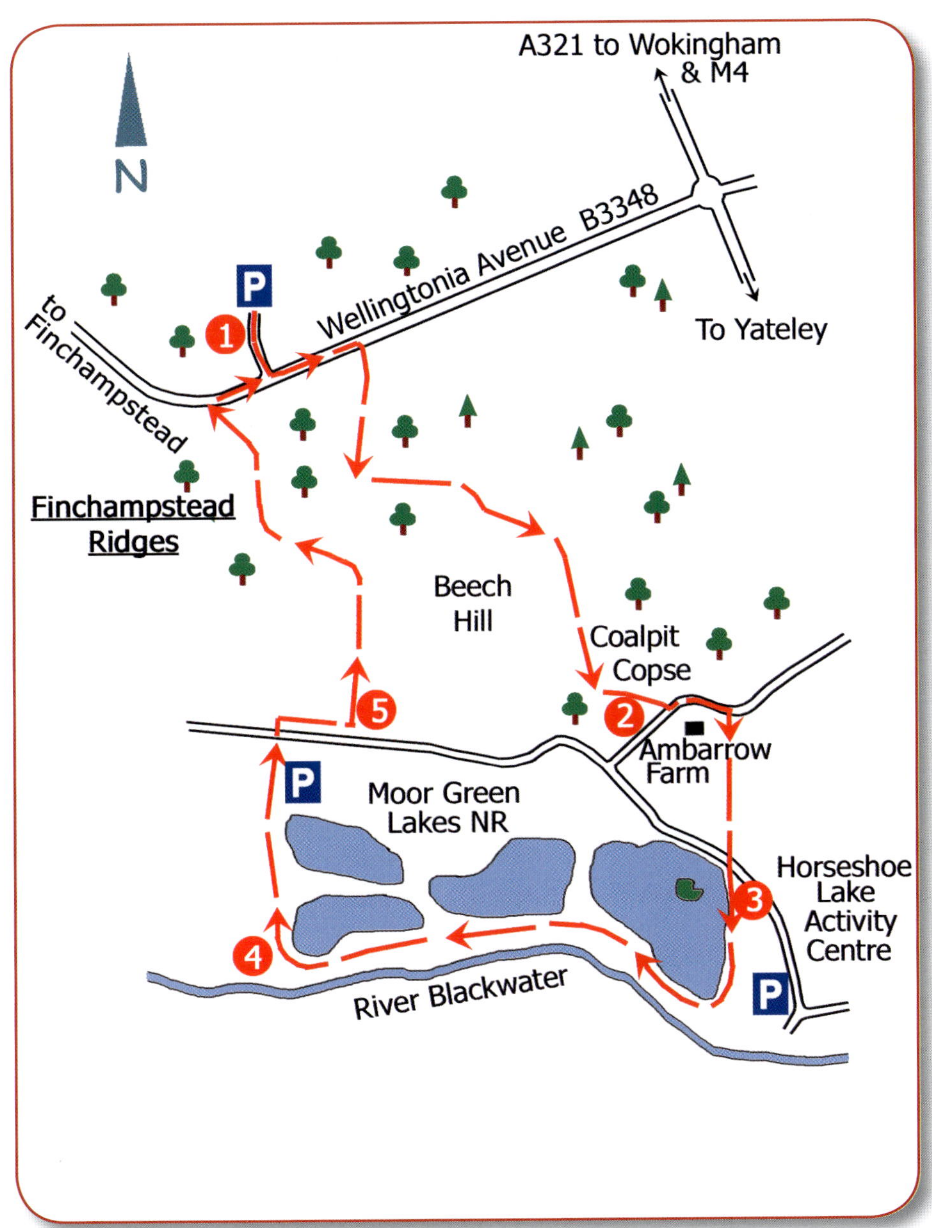

N
A321 to Wokingham & M4
To Yateley
Wellingtonia Avenue B3348
P
1
to Finchampstead
Finchampstead Ridges
Beech Hill
Coalpit Copse
2
Ambarrow Farm
5
P
Moor Green Lakes NR
Horseshoe Lake Activity Centre
3
P
4
River Blackwater

a quiet residential road. There are no pavements, so walk along the wide grass verge at the side of the road.

5 Just by Moor Green House, turn left to follow the Restricted Byway. The path leads gently uphill, passing an old thatched cottage on your right. Turn left at a wooden gate into Finchampstead Ridges, passing the National Trust sign on your left. Follow the winding woodland path ahead. At a junction of paths, turn right to follow the permitted footpath sign steeply uphill through the pine trees. At the top, there is a welcome bench where you can sit and admire the fantastic view. When you are ready, continue ahead passing oak trees, and walk towards the road. Pass a stone monument on your left. Turn right at Wellingtonia Avenue and walk roadside on the grass verge, then cross the road with care when the pavement starts. The car park is on your left.

◆ Background Notes ◆

Heathlands are not a natural habitat. They were created by our ancestors thousands of years ago as they cleared away the forest for wood and to create land for grazing. The National Trust owns 60 acres around Finchampstead Ridges. It is removing some of the pine and invasive rhododendron, in order to create the ideal growing conditions for heather and gorse, which thrive in this acidic, open environment. Finchampstead Ridges are known for their amazing views over Berkshire, Surrey and Hampshire. There is a bench near the end of the walk where you can stop for a well-earned rest and enjoy the panorama before you.

Moor Green Lakes Nature Reserve is another landscape that was created by man, although more recently, as the lakes were once open pits for gravel extraction. When this industry ended, the pits filled with water to create the tranquil lakes that you walk past. They have been colonised by a variety of waterside vegetation, which in turn has made the area an important site for breeding and wintering water birds. It has been a nature reserve since 1993 and in this time over 200 different species of bird have been recorded in the area.

Swinley Forest, Bracknell
Exploring Woodland Trails

Swinley Forest at Bracknell is an excellent base for a day out. There are 2,500 acres of forest leading from the car park, as well as adventure playgrounds and a hands-on science exhibition. Despite its size, it is hard to get lost as there are signed trails taking you off in various directions, with handy signposts pointing the way back to the car park if you get tired. The area is very popular with mountain bikers and bike hire is available next to the Discovery Centre if you want to travel at a faster speed. This walk follows part of the nature trail to visit the peaceful waters of Mill Pond and an area of mixed woodland, before returning through the forest along the wide, tree-lined main track.

Getting there From junction 10 of the M4, follow the A322 through Bracknell. Turn off westwards on the B3430 and follow the brown tourist signs for the Look Out Discovery Centre. The entrance is opposite the Coral Reef swimming pool.

Length of walk 2 miles.
Time 2 hours.
Terrain Easy walking along wide woodland tracks, although the smaller paths near the Mill Pond can be boggy in wet weather. The main paths are suitable for all-terrain pushchairs.
Start/Parking There is a large free car park by the Look Out Discovery Centre (GR: SU 877662).
Map OS Explorer 160 Windsor, Weybridge & Bracknell.
Refreshments A coffee shop sells hot and cold drinks, snacks and ice creams. There are also lots of picnic tables by the playgrounds where you can stop for a drink and watch your children play.

The Walk

1 From the car park, follow the sign for Go Ape! Pass the Go Ape! ticket office on your left and walk straight on, heading east. The path crosses a small forest stream at one point. Continue along the path until you come to

◆ Fun Things to See and Do ◆

There are two large **adventure playgrounds** by the car park, one for older and the other for younger children.

Most of the forest is filled with **Scots pine**, but there are also **birch, beech, sweet chestnut and oak**. As you walk, see which parts of the forest are darker – the evergreen conifers or the deciduous mixed woodland. Also have a look at the woodland floor in these two different areas to see which different plants and fungi you can find in the contrasting habitats. See how many **different leaves** your child can collect then find and identify the trees they came from. In autumn, there are acorns, conkers and pine cones to collect.

Old Bracknell Road. Cross with care, there is the occasional car, and follow the path opposite, signed 'Mill Pond Nature Trail'.

This path first heads towards the A322, then leads you to the right along Mill Ride, heading south through a pretty area of mixed

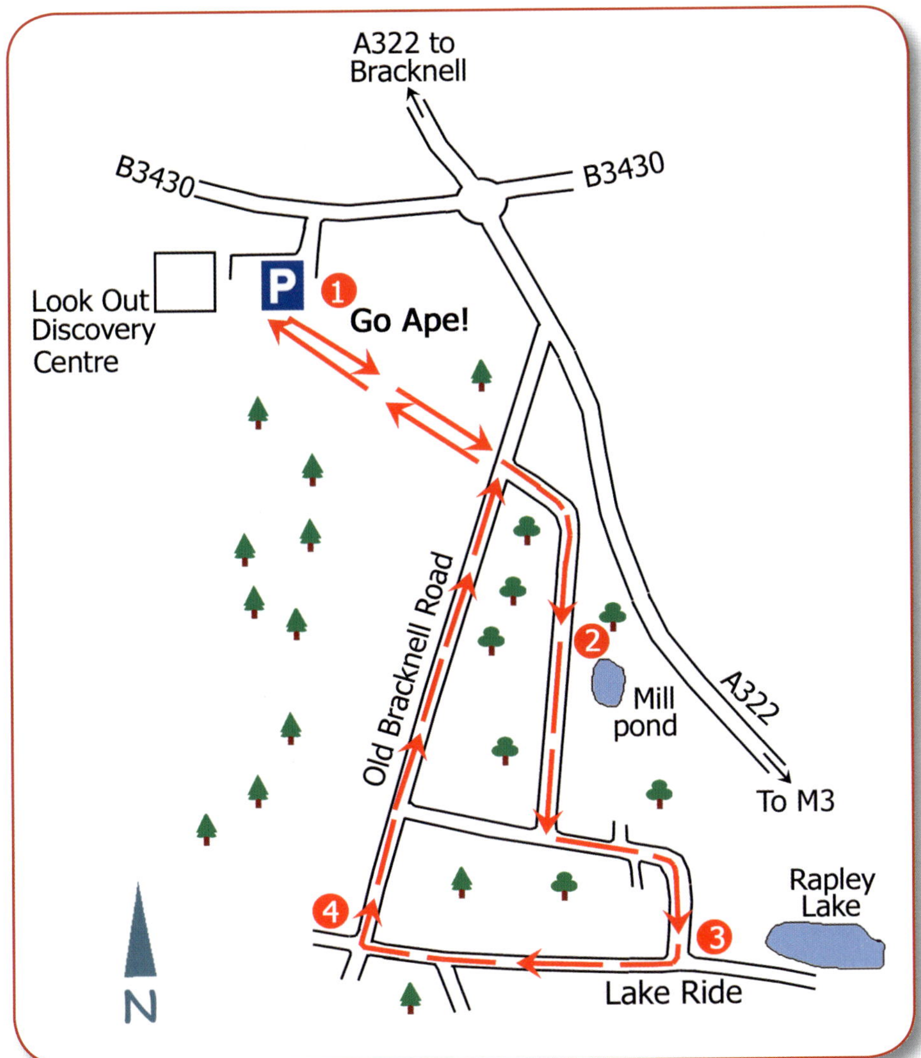

woodland. As you go gently downhill, small brooks then thick bracken border the path. Watch out for a path on your left signed to the Mill Pond.

2 It is well worth taking a detour here by following the woodland path on your left to see the pond; otherwise continue straight on. At the end of the main path, turn left to head east downhill on a wide track. Ignore a path on your left and right, to continue straight on along this track, passing a Swinley Forest sign on your right. The path veers round to the right, to take you through some large rhododendron bushes. This path ends at a T-junction with Lake Ride. If you want to see Rapley Lake, turn left here and continue along the path to the lake, before returning to this point. This would add just under ¼ mile to the walk.

3 Otherwise turn right and walk along the ride. There are often parked cars ahead of you as the paths on your left form a special mountain bike trail. Continue ahead, passing a wide grassy path that crosses your route, until you come to a junction and signpost.

4 Now head right, following the sign for Old Bracknell Road and The Look Out. There are lots of massive sweet chestnut trees further along this road with beautifully fissured bark on their trunks. You will find their spiny-cased nuts on the ground beneath them. As you head along the road, eventually you come to the signpost that you passed in point 1 of the walk. Turn left here and retrace your steps back to the car park.

The still waters of Mill Pond reflect the surrounding trees.

◆ Background Notes ◆

It is well worth visiting the **Look Out Discovery Centre** after the walk. It has various rooms filled with hands-on interactive science and nature exhibits. Younger children will enjoy pushing the buttons to see what happens next, while there are explanations for older children to learn about the science behind what they see. There is also a high tower that you can climb to get a bird's-eye view of the forest. By the entrance there is a large gift shop and tourist information area. Go to www.bracknell-forest.gov.uk/be for prices and opening times or telephone 01344 354400.

Braywick Park, Maidenhead
A Tree Trail & Nature Reserve

Braywick Park is an excellent family day out. Children can run from tree to tree in the Formal Park following the Tree Trail. The trail includes a mix of conifers and native deciduous trees, with different leaves and interesting cones to collect. Then after walking through the nature reserve, there are two fantastic play areas by the sports fields that your children won't want to leave. Braywick Park is clearly marked out with posts to direct you around the route and for younger families there are a few short cuts if small legs are getting tired. Although you are only minutes from Maidenhead, when you stand in the centre of the nature reserve, you won't be able to see a single house.

Getting there Braywick Park is just off the A308 (Braywick Road). From junction 8/9 of the M4, follow the A308 towards Maidenhead. Turn right down Hibbert Road and Braywick Nature Centre is on your left. If you are using public transport, Maidenhead railway station is just north of the park (GR: SU 888808).

Length of walk 1½ miles.
Time 1½ hours.
Terrain The paths are flat and grassy with some steps. The Tree Trail and The Dell are suitable for toddlers and buggies.
Start/Parking There is a free car park by the Nature Centre in Hibbert Road directly in front of the Formal Park and Tree Trail (GR: SU 895795).

Maps OS Explorer 160 Windsor, Weybridge & Bracknell and OS Explorer 172 Chiltern Hills East.
Refreshments There is a restaurant by the sports fields and lots of benches along the route where you could stop for a picnic.

The Walk

1 Follow the path round the Formal Park to see the trees. At the eastern edge of the park, take the stone steps down to a pretty wildlife pond. If you have a buggy, there is a sloped path further along to the right of the steps. Although the pond looks as if it has always been here, it was actually created in the 1990s to provide a different habitat for wildlife. Cross the small bridge over the pond and find the last three trees from the Tree Trail. Pass a post with number '2' from

◆ Fun Things to See and Do ◆

There are lots of different species of trees in Braywick Park. The **Tree Trail** leads you around the Formal Park and The Dell to discover twelve of these trees. There are leaflets telling you all about the trail by the Nature Centre. The first two trees are an Oriental plane and a western red cedar. Then follow the path clockwise to find a Scots pine, European lime, Norway maple, monkey puzzle, red oak, walnut and Wellingtonia. You find the last three trees in The Dell: a conifer called coast redwood, an English oak and a beech tree.

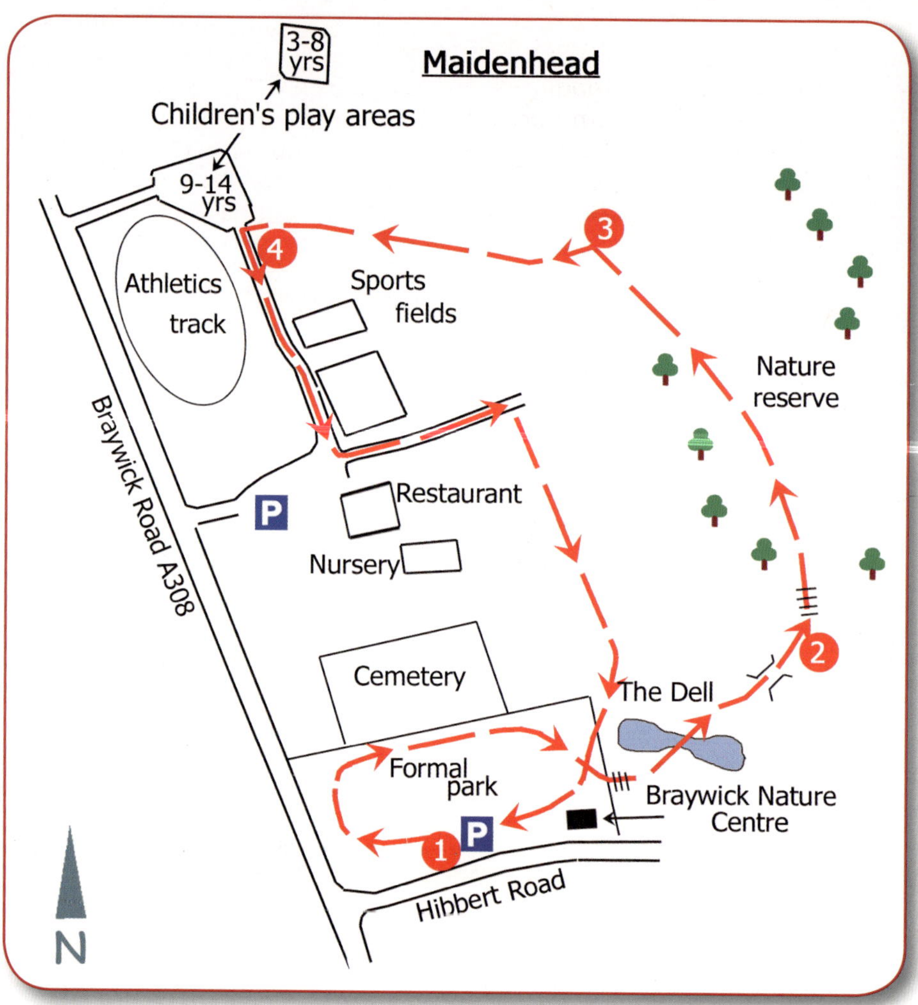

the Park Trail on your right. Then ignore a turn to your left and continue straight on towards the nature reserve, passing an information sign, and cross the bridge.

2 Ignore the turn to your left and follow the sign towards The Cut. There is a large colourful board labelled *Grasslands*, showing the wildlife that lives in the area. Take the steps on your left here and go up into the nature reserve. Walk through a small patch of native woodland before coming out into an open grassy area. There are lovely views from here across the park and you can sometimes spot red kites soaring in the sky and butterflies in high summer. Walk ahead across the field, veering slightly left, until you reach a Braywick Park Trail post '5'.

3 Turn left and follow the path downhill to a green sign. Here you cross Green Lane, an old track that runs from Bray to Cookham. Go straight ahead onto Braywick Sports Ground. The path to your left leads back to The Dell if you want to shorten the route. But to visit the two play areas, walk ahead following the edge of the sports fields.

4 When you can persuade your children to leave the play areas, walk along the path to pass the WAMDSAD building and pavilion on your left then go past the fenced football pitches. Just before the restaurant and plant nursery, turn left along a small road that leads towards the sports fields. Turn right at the end of this road and walk across the sports fields towards the left corner of the hedge in front of you. The grass has been left longer here to encourage grasshoppers and crickets, as well as small mammals like shrews and voles. Go through the gap in the hedge and continue ahead, passing a couple of benches and a picnic table on your right. At a signpost turn right to follow the tarmac path back towards the car park.

◆ Background Notes ◆

Archaeologists have found flint working from Mesolithic man at Braywick, proving it to be one of the **earliest settled places in the Thames Valley**. Pottery from Neolithic man found in the area from around 3,340 BC is the earliest ever to be discovered in Britain. When you arrive in the car park, you are standing on the site of the 18th-century **Braywick Lodge**, knocked down in 1969. Luckily, its grounds have been preserved to form part of the Tree Trail and include the Formal Park and The Dell. The Nature Centre was converted from its stable block.

Cookham

Watch Out for Mole, Ratty, Badger and Toad

Cookham is a fascinating village to explore and sits by one of the most glorious stretches of the River Thames. It was home and inspiration to the artist Sir Stanley Spencer and the author Kenneth Grahame. The walk starts by following a section of the Thames Path. Across the river you can see lavish villas, their manicured gardens leading down to private boat houses, before the countryside opens up with water meadows and willow trees. The second half of the route leaves the Thames to walk through Cock Marsh, following the edge of a steep chalk hillside. These peaceful water meadows have been owned by the National Trust since 1934 and are a Site of Special Scientific Interest. Look out for the Bronze Age bowl barrows as you walk.

Getting there Cookham lies on the A4094 to the north of Maidenhead. Heading east out of Maidenhead on the A4, turn left onto the A4094. As you reach Cookham, turn left onto School Lane, then left again onto the B4447. If coming from the north, turn right onto High Street. The car park is on your right. Cookham rail station is further west along this road.

Length of walk 3½ miles.
Time 3 hours.
Terrain Level walking along pavements and unsurfaced paths.
Start/Parking There is a free National Trust car park by the edge of Cookham Moor on the B4447 (GR: SU 895854).
Map OS Explorer 172 Chiltern Hills East.
Refreshments Halfway through the walk you pass the Bounty pub; its large beer garden and children's play equipment make it a good spot to stop for a break.

The Walk

1 Follow the public footpath across Cookham Moor towards the village, passing the Crown on your left. As you walk down the historic High Street, look out for a blue plaque on your right marking Sir Stanley Spencer's house. When you get to a junction, turn left, heading towards the church. Turn left down Church Gate and walk into the churchyard of Holy Trinity. If your children are fans of *Doctor Who*, they will be enthralled by the 'Crying Angel' by the entrance. Spencer was equally fascinated by this stone angel and it is depicted in some of his paintings. The path leads through the churchyard to the Thames. Turn left and follow the footpath.

2 Bell Rope Meadow on your left was once used by rope makers. At the edge of the meadow turn left to follow the footpath away from the Thames. At the end of the path go through a metal gate then directly right and through a wooden kissing gate, to follow the public footpath back to the river, passing the sailing club on your right. Continue along the Thames Path, passing the occasional row of pollarded willows, until you come to another gate. The path leads under Bourne End railway bridge. The Thames Path crosses over the bridge here, but this walk continues along the south bank of the river, soon passing the Bounty pub.

3 Pass houses and a swing gate into an open field and continue walking by the river, passing through another swing gate and an arable field. Eventually you come to the white Ferry Cottage. Here the path leaves the river behind to head across the field towards a prominent hill in front of you. Follow the grassy footpath towards a footpath sign. When you get to the sign, follow the footpath left across an arable field towards the hill. Go through a gate and when you get to the base of the hill turn left.

4 Walk with the hill on your right. You can just see the sails of the boats as they drift down the Thames on your left. Go through a swing gate and head down towards a railway bridge, then through a kissing gate and under the bridge. When you come to a cattle grid turn

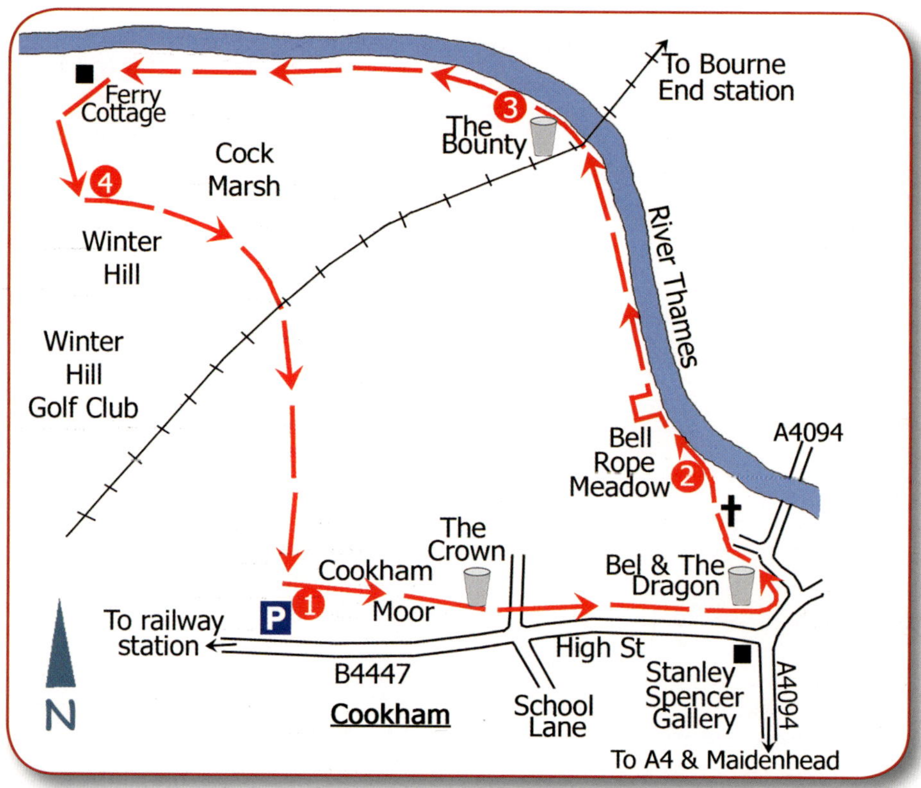

◆ Fun Things to See and Do ◆

The **Swan Upping Ceremony** takes place in July. It dates back over 600 years to medieval times, when swans were a prized food at royal banquets. Now the Royal Swan Marker catches the new cygnets to count, measure, weigh and mark them. The Queen's Swan Uppers, resplendent in scarlet uniforms with flags and pennants, set out from Sunbury and row 70 miles down the Thames to Abingdon in six traditional skiffs. When they spot a swan, they shout 'All up', which gives the ceremony its name. Children will enjoy **watching** people 'simply messing about in boats'. They can also **feed the swans**, if they aren't otherwise engaged with their royal health check.

right to follow the Chiltern Way, with a golf course on your right. Follow the path straight on. Pass Pound Farm on your right and cross a small footbridge into the car park.

◆ Background Notes ◆

The renowned 20th-century painter **Stanley Spencer** spent most of his life in Cookham. He loved the village so much that while studying at the Slade School of Fine Art in London, his friends nicknamed him 'Cookham'. A former church in the centre of Cookham has been converted into an informative gallery of his work, much of which was inspired by the scenery that you are about to walk through. It is free for children under 16. Spencer is buried in Cookham churchyard.

Kenneth Grahame was born in Scotland, but spent his childhood in Cookham, where he lived with his grandmother. He returned to the area with his wife and small son to write the children's classic *The Wind in the Willows* (1908). The adventures of Ratty, Mole, Mr Badger and Mr Toad on and around the river were inspired by the tranquil scenery around him. **The River and Rowing Museum** in nearby Henley-on-Thames has a permanent *Wind in the Willows* exhibition, as well as a gallery about the Thames (www.rrm.co.uk).

Eton

A Famous College in an Ancient Town

The viewing tower and stainless steel bollards were designed by Wendy Ramshaw

This walk takes you on a historic stroll down Eton High Street with lots to look at along the way, as well as tempting shops and timber-framed pubs and restaurants. The end of the High Street is dominated by the majestic buildings of Eton College itself. The second half of the walk returns to the Thames Path as you walk across The Brocas to the bridge, with stunning views of Windsor Castle across the river. The Windsor walk also passes this bridge, so if you wanted to explore further, you could link the two walks and continue into Windsor.

Getting there Eton is one mile south of junction 6 on the M4; take the A355 into Windsor, if approaching from the motorway. Follow the signs for long-stay car parks. Windsor and Eton Riverside train station is at the start of this walk.

Length of walk 1½ miles.

Time 2 hours, longer if you are going on a guided tour of the college.

Terrain Pavements and level grass make this walk suitable for all-terrain pushchairs, although there is a short flight of steps from Thames Side up to the bridge.

Start/Parking The walk starts from Windsor and Eton Riverside car park by the train station, which has over 100 parking places (GR: SU 968773).

Map OS Explorer 160 Windsor, Weybridge & Bracknell.

Refreshments Eton High Street is full of tempting places to eat. The Brocas is a perfect picnic spot.

The Walk

1 At the entrance to the car park, there is an opening by the River House restaurant. Go through this and turn right to the River Thames. Then turn left and walk along Thames Side to Windsor Bridge. Cross the bridge into Eton, pausing to admire the stunning view down the Thames on either side of you.

2 At the end of the bridge you pass a row of five stainless steel bollards and a viewing tower, which were specially commissioned for 2000 to mark the entrance to Eton. Walk ahead onto the High Street. This busy

◆ Fun Things to See and Do ◆

Challenge your children to **spot the following** on Eton High Street: wooden stocks, an insurance certificate from the Sun Insurance Co (the firemen wanted to check they'd be paid before putting out the fire), a Victorian metal post box, the Eton College school motto, *Floreat Etona* – Let Eton flourish – with three lily flowers forming part of Eton's coat of arms, and the royal coat of arms above a shop door.

Walking back across The Brocas with a panoramic view of Windsor Castle

street is filled with antique shops, gift shops and timber-framed pubs and restaurants. Cross Baldwin's Bridge and look down Gulliver's Passage on the left to see a cast of a section of the Parthenon frieze. Then walk on to see the impressive buildings of Eton College.

3 Eton playing fields are at the end of this street, north of the college buildings, and there are public footpaths if you want to have a look at them. But this walk now heads west down Keats Lane to join the Thames Path. Keats Lane is next to Eton library on the left of the road. The road sign is rather hard to spot, so look out for a sign on the wall that says 'B3026 Maidenhead'. Go straight on down this lane, ignoring a right turn down Eton Wick Road, and follow the sign for Swan Lifeline. Pass Eton College Natural History Museum on your left and the rather decrepit but beautiful door to Eton College music department on your right, with the Eton College coat of arms above it. You then come to a playing field on your left and a public footpath sign. There is a small children's play area on the right here.

4 Walk left into the playing fields and turn right to follow the hedge. This part of the walk offers spectacular views of Windsor Castle, which looks particularly magical when lit by the late afternoon sun. Go through a gap in the fence then cross Meadow Lane. Follow the public footpath sign by the side of a metal five bar gate and go into The Brocas.

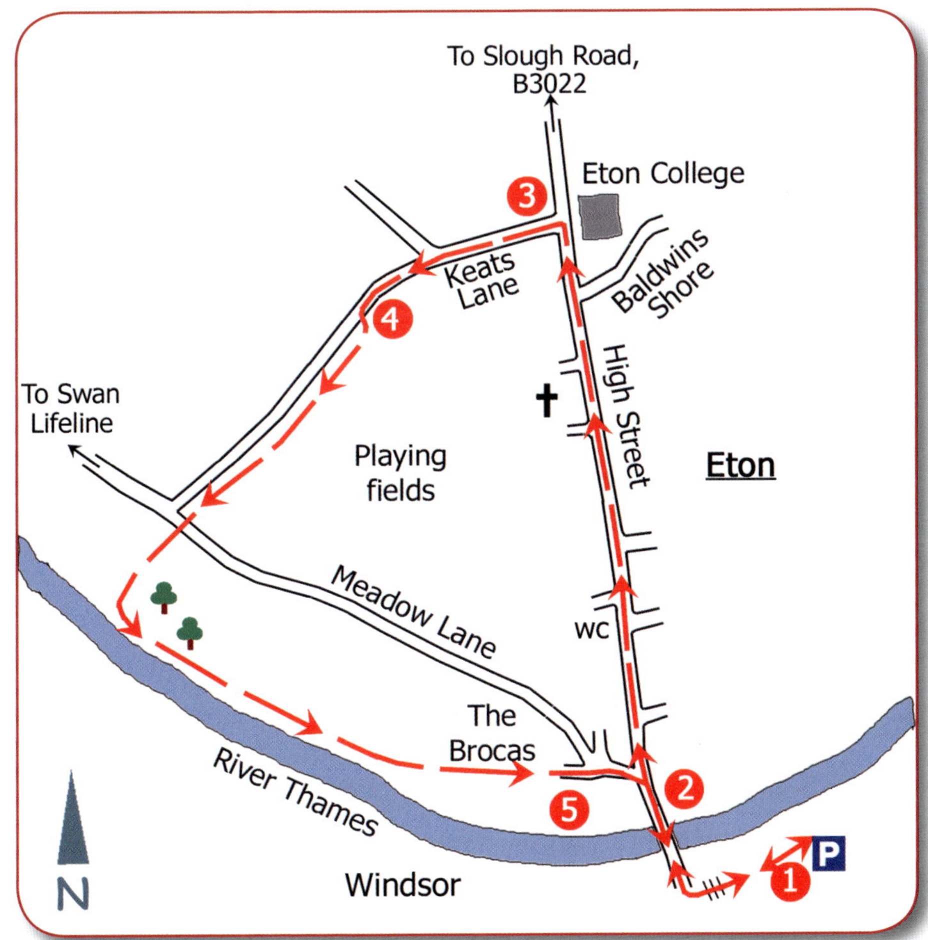

Walk towards the trees to reach the River Thames. Now turn left to follow the Thames Path with views to Alexandra Gardens on the other side of the river and Windsor Castle ahead.

5 Go through a gate at the end of The Brocas to walk past Eton College Boathouse, then walk down Brocas Street to return to Windsor Bridge. Turn right and retrace your steps over the bridge. Now you can either turn left and walk back to the car park, or go right to explore Alexandra Gardens and the Windsor walk, which passes this exact spot.

◆ Background Notes ◆

Eton College is the most famous public school in the world. It was founded in 1440 by King Henry VI for the education of the poor. School life by the mid-16th century was a grim affair. The boys would sleep three to a bed, with lessons starting at 6 am. Fridays were a day of fasting when they could eat nothing at all. The year was divided into two halves, with the boys only allowed home for a three-week summer holiday. About the only similarity that a modern Etonian would recognise is that the terms are still called halves, despite there now being three of them. Princes William and Harry both attended Eton, as well as twenty prime ministers, including David Cameron. Sadly for the tourists, the uniform no longer consists of a top hat and walking cane, but they do still wear a black tailcoat, waistcoat and pinstriped trousers. If you are a senior boy who has done particularly well, you get to wear a wing collar and white bow tie. I imagine most boys would struggle to see how this could be considered a treat. You can be shown round the college buildings if you pre-book on a one hour guided tour. Look on the Eton College website (www.etoncollege. com/VisitsToEton.aspx) for details.

Swan Lifeline is a charitable organisation, founded in 1984, to look after sick and injured swans. Initially the group worked from their own homes, but in 1992 Eton College gave them the free lease of Cuckoo Weir. They hold an annual open day when you can look round. Check their website for details (www.swanlifeline.org.uk) or telephone 01753 859397.

20

Windsor

Home to a Queen

Church Street has cafés and the smallest park in Windsor

Windsor is an exciting place for children to explore. The castle dominates the centre of town; with its arrow slit windows, towers and battlements it could be taken straight from the pages of a fairy tale. The fact that a real queen might actually be sitting the other side of the towering stone walls only adds to the adventure. The walk weaves through the cobbled streets surrounding the castle before leading down to Windsor Great Park, to see 'The Long Walk' disappearing over the horizon. However, this walk heads back past the castle, passing the Royal Mews on the way, to feed the swans by the side of the Thames. At this point you could continue over the bridge to explore Eton, or walk through Alexandra Gardens to return to the start of the walk via the Royal Windsor maze.

Getting there Windsor is one mile south of junction 6 on the M4. As you head into Windsor (on the A355 if coming from the motorway), follow the signs for long-stay car parks. There are lots of multi-storey and open-air car parks, with the long-stay ones a cheaper option for all-day parking. The car park by Windsor and Eton Riverside station (GR: SU 968773) is recommended for this walk. Public transport links are good with two train stations and a frequent bus service into town.

Length of walk 1 mile.
Time 2 hours.
Terrain Level pavements, cobbled paths and some steps.
Start/Parking The car park by Windsor and Eton Riverside station is just a 10-minute walk away from the town centre. The walk starts at the entrance to the Royal Windsor Shopping Centre which sits in a Grade II listed Victorian railway station opposite the castle on Thames Street. (GR: SU 966769).
Map OS Explorer 160 Windsor, Weybridge & Bracknell.
Refreshments A café, pub or restaurant is never far from you on this walk and lots of them have tables outside where you can sit and watch the world stroll by. Windsor Great Park is also a perfect spot for a picnic, as well as giving small legs a rest in the middle of the walk.

The Walk

1 Start at the entrance to the Royal Windsor Shopping Centre and walk right towards the castle. Cross Peascod Street then go over the pedestrian crossing and up Castle Hill to see the impressive castle gateway. Turn right down Church Street, looking out for Nell Gwynne's house and the tiny Church Street Gardens. At the end of Church Street turn right, then right again down Market Street. Turn left at 'The Crooked House of Windsor' and count how many steps it takes to walk down Queen Charlotte Street. There is a plaque on the corner claiming that at 51 feet 10 inches it is the smallest street in Britain. There is a water fountain at the end of the street to commemorate the Queen's Silver Jubilee in 1977 and from this point you can really see how much the crooked house, built in 1687 from unseasoned oak, leans over the street. Now walk under

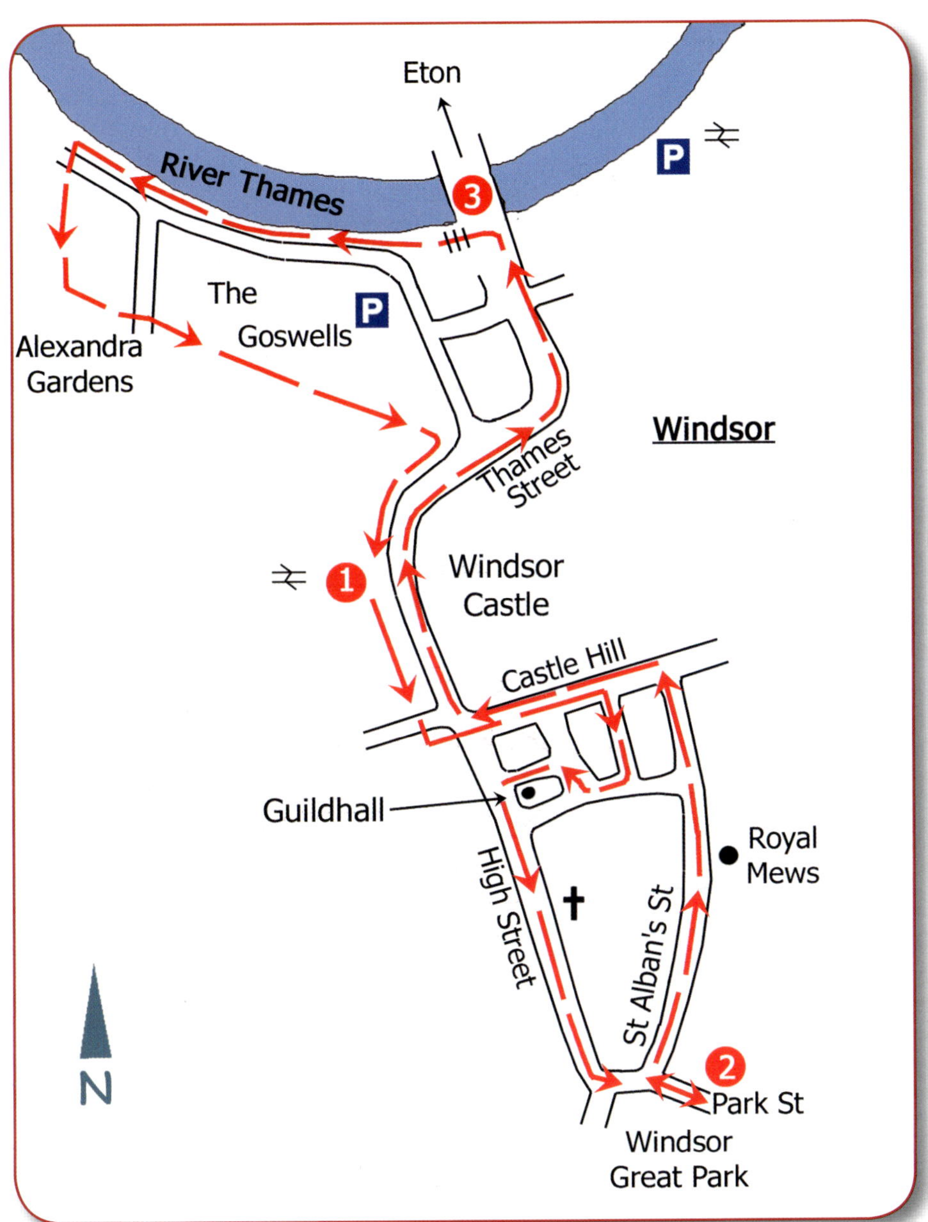
Eton
River Thames
3
P
P
The Goswells
P
Alexandra Gardens
Windsor
Thames Street
Windsor Castle
1
Castle Hill
Guildhall
Royal Mews
High Street
St Alban's St
2
Park St
Windsor Great Park
N

the columns of the Windsor Guildhall, making sure you look up to see the four shorter columns in the centre. Continue down High Street, passing Windsor parish church on your left. Then cross the road to Park Street and the imposing entrance to Windsor Great Park.

2 The Long Walk disappears off to your right while on your left you can peer through the gates at the guard on duty outside Windsor Castle. When you are ready to leave the park, retrace your steps back down Park Street. At the blue post box veer right down St Alban's Street, passing

◆ Fun Things to See and Do ◆

Windsor is such a famous, historic town that it is packed with interesting **things to spot**. See if you can find the following as you walk: a large statue of Queen Victoria, a horse-drawn cart taking tourists on a trip, two royal coats of arms – one in stone and one in colour – a fireplace in a garden wall, a copy of King Charles I's death warrant signed by Oliver Cromwell, a bright blue post box, a bust of King Edward VII (ER VII) above an alleyway and a glazed arrow slit window.

Along the walk you will find a hopscotch game in Church Street Gardens; this shows the shields of some of the monarchs. Alexandra Gardens has a play area and a large sundial where you can stand on the month to find the time. In The Goswells there is a large brick maze to run through, jumping over various chess pieces as you go before landing on the castle in the middle.

The **Guards** march up the High Street and into the castle at around 10.50 am every day in the summer and alternate days in the winter, but never on a Sunday. The schedule is set by the British Army and can change, so check online before you set off, to avoid disappointment (www.windsor.gov.uk). The changing of the guard ceremony happens inside the castle and is included in the castle admission price.

a well on your left and the entrances to the Royal Mews on your right. The high green gates are to allow the carriages to fit through them. At the end of the road turn left down Castle Hill then right onto High Street. This street curves round the castle walls as Curfew Tower looms up right next to you. Under the tower are the dungeons where prisoners were kept before their execution. Their bodies were then hanged from the tower as a warning to others. The road leads down to a statue of Christian Victor, a grandson of Queen Victoria. Stop to count his many medals; the key on the left of the statue tells you what each medal was for. Cross the road at the traffic lights and stay on Thames Street as it leads to the river, passing the family home of Sir Christopher Wren.

3 Stop to admire the view down the Thames from Windsor Bridge. You could continue over the bridge to explore the Eton walk, or go down the steps on the left to walk along Jennings Wharf. When you are opposite the Royal Windsor Wheel, there are steps and a slope leading up to the pavement. Cross the road with care into Alexandra Gardens; the play area is over to your right. Then walk towards the castle, passing the sundial as you leave the park, and cross the road at the lights. Now walk through The Goswells, a former Victorian slum, with a brick maze on your right. Walk straight ahead through the park and down Boots Passage. Then go up the steps and stop to admire the tiled map of Windsor on your left. Turn right and retrace your steps along Thames Street to the start of the walk.

◆ Background Notes ◆

There has been a castle at Windsor since the time of William the Conqueror. He built a wooden motte and bailey castle here between 1070 and 1086. This makes **Windsor Castle** the oldest and largest continuously inhabited castle in the world. Windsor Castle is an official residence of the Queen and she is at home when the Royal Standard flies over the Round Tower; if it is the Union Jack fluttering in the wind then she is away.

Windsor Guildhall dates from 1687 and cost £2,000 to build. It was designed by Sir Thomas Fiddes, but he died before it was completed and the famous architect Sir Christopher Wren took over for the last two years of its construction. The town councillors insisted on the extra four pillars in the centre of the ground floor, as they didn't believe that there were enough columns to support the weight of the rooms above. Wren was so annoyed with this unnecessary change that he made these four columns an inch short of the ceiling. This is a popular spot for weddings and in 2005 it was used for two very different celebrations – the royal wedding of HRH Prince Charles to Camilla Parker-Bowles and the civil partnership of Sir Elton John and David Furnish.